DARE TO BE
DIFFERENT,
FREE TO BE
YOURSELF

DARE TO BE
DIFFERENT,
FREE TO BE
YOURSELF

DEANN HUMMEL

DARE TO BE DIFFERENT, FREE TO BE YOURSELF

Scripture quotations marked NIV are taken from the Holy Bible, New International Version®. NIV®. Copyright © 1973, 1978, 1984 by International Bible Society. Used by permission of Zondervan. All rights reserved. [Biblica]

iUniverse books may be ordered through booksellers or by contacting:

iUniverse
1663 Liberty Drive
Bloomington, IN 47403
www.iuniverse.com
1-800-Authors (1-800-288-4677)

ISBN: 978-1-5320-3343-8 (sc)
ISBN: 978-1-5320-3344-5 (e)

Library of Congress Control Number: 2017916145

Print information available on the last page.

iUniverse rev. date: 10/27/2017

Contents

Dare to Be Different—Be the Real You!............................ vii

Introduction xi

An Overview xv

  1. Pretend 1
  2. The Unrealistic Perfection 3
  3. Brand-New Day 7
  4. Notes from Above 12
  5. Believe What's in Your Heart 14
  6. Life 17
  7. To Live Out Loud Takes Courage 18
  8. Things to Ponder—Peaceful Easy Living............22
  9. Puppet Strings 32
  10. Selfish and Mean 34
  11. Hurt 36
  12. Heart Feels..40
  13. It's about Forgiveness 44
  14. No Looking Back 48
  15. Love 50
  16. No One Can Come Close to the Real You but You....52
  17. Embrace Your Flaws—We All Have Them............54
  18. No One Can Come Closer than Me......................59
  19. Angels from Above 61
  20. Hope 63
  21. Yourself 71
  22. Your Future Shining Bright.................................73

23. Best Medicine 75

24. Respect Yourself 77

25. "Be Yourself" 88

26. Lord, It's All about You 106

27. Be Yourself 108

28. Clothes 111

29. The Faith 112

30. Celebrate Life 116

31. Carnival Ride 118

32. Choice 120

33. Things Happen 122

34. Meaning 127

35. "Things Happen." 132

36. Friendship 137

37. A Story of Trust 140

38. Change Takes Action 147

39. The Finish Line 152

40. Ending 154

DARE TO BE DIFFERENT— BE THE REAL YOU!

Bees will be abuzz when the real you is in action.
Dare to let the light in and shine through you.

Let the love in; it will mend what is broken. The action has taken place. It will make you whole again through his love, as it has been spoken, as you walk in it.

The sunshine through the rain—as the flowers will bloom, so will you. The real you will be in full bloom where it has been buried for so long.

Ready to come out and shine, you have almost reached the surface and are peeking through.

It's a matter of trust and faith, and hope and love have a lot to do with how you view yourself and others. But most of all, love because if you don't love yourself or even like yourself, how will you like or love others? When you don't love yourself, you can't give love to someone else. You can't give away what you don't have.

Take a look at your life and how has it been going. What's your life like right now? Most of all, how do you treat yourself? Do you respect yourself? Do you love and like yourself? Did you answer no to the last two questions? If so, how did that make you feel? (Not great, I'll bet.) Look at it like this when you do that to yourself: How are others supposed to treat you when you treat yourself that way? That's not right, because as the Bible says, "Do unto others as you would have them do unto you." In other words, love others as you love yourself.

So if you don't treat yourself right, how can you treat others right? When you don't love yourself, how can you expect others to love you?

You allow others to hurt you because that's what you have always done. You take it on yourself, and you blame yourself for others' actions and choices that you think are your responsibility. That's unrealistic for you to think you need to take it on yourself.

The truth is that everyone needs to take responsibility for his or her own actions and the choices that he or she makes in life. You want to blame others and hand over your troubles for someone else to deal with them; you do not want to own up to them. We need to accept that the choices and mistakes we make are no one else's but our own. We all have consciences to live with after we make choices. Some choices are good, and some are not so good, but we learn from all of them. Some leave scars, and some leave heartache and pain. It isn't right to put the blame on others for our mistakes and choices. It will hurt you even more than you realize to take over someone else's job. We have our own responsibilities to handle.

Punishing yourself for someone's mistakes is wrong. You punish yourself even more when you try to fix someone else's mistake. Why put yourself through that self-punishment for no reason except your own mission of self-destruction?

It is the worst punishment you can put on yourself, taking on something you have no business doing in the first place. Because you are so afraid to face your own responsibilities, you put your nose into someone else's business. You try to fix someone else's mess when you have your own to deal with.

Let it go; don't do it one more minute. You are in charge of your own responsibilities. Do not to hand them over to someone else to deal with.

Deal with them now, or deal with them later, but remember you will have to deal with them sooner or later. It's your own responsibility, not someone else's, to make sense of them. Deal with your responsibilities, and let others deal with theirs. You'll be better off, and others will be too. Stop trying to fix everyone's problems that they don't want to take responsibility for; it's not yours to fix.

Don't put guilt and shame on yourself and cause pain to yourself; it's not your job to make others happy all the time. Stop wasting time on doing someone's job. Take responsibility for your own actions, and let others take care of their own.

Once you realize we all have our own pain to go through, and you're trying to punish others for your pain, the only one who gets hurt in the long run is you. But the truth is, we all need to face our pain at one time or another to be free of it once and for all.

It seems hard at times while you are still carrying around the pain. Talk to God, and confess the reason behind the pain you've carried, and give it all to him. He will show you the why behind it and will help you through it. Then you will begin to mend.

Being you is so rewarding and is so much easier than trying to be something you are not.

God already knows how special you are because he made you and is pleased with you, even when you make mistakes. We all make them every now and then, and that's okay. Talk to God; he will forgive you. All you have to do is ask, and it will be done. Remember you need to do the asking. He knows what you are thinking, but you have to ask first, and then he will forgive. It's that simple. Our minds think it is going to be so hard, but it really isn't. It is a lot easier than we think. Our minds read too much into it and make it a lot harder than it is. It comes down to this: we make it harder to forgive ourselves than others. We put ourselves under so much pressure to be perfect, and when we are not, we really punish ourselves. Let it go, and let yourself off the hook. Forgive yourself, love yourself and others, be true to yourself, and don't compromise yourself or get back at others.

It isn't worth all that unnecessary pain. In the end, the only one who gets hurt and pays is you. Why try to fix something you cannot? What is done is done; move on from there. You can't change something that has already happened. Forgive yourself, move on, and learn from it; God forgave you. Why not forgive yourself?

It starts with you and ends with you. Why not enjoy the real you? God attended us too. Why not be the real you, not pretend you never make mistakes or claim never to make them? It's okay to make mistakes; that's not living if you don't make any. It is real living when you do; you know you are learning each and every day.

So don't beat yourself up when you make mistakes because we all make them. Give yourself permission to let the walls of perfection down, and be the real you. Have fun along the way. Let your hair down; you've been way too uptight for way too long.

Running in the rain and getting wet is okay. There is no blueprint for how long you can run in the rain. Take a few others when you go in the rain. Don't live an uptight life, always with your panties in a bunch, always in a crunch to make everything just so. Nothing has to be perfect to be right.

Know in your heart you are living right because it is right when you are living from the inside out. When you live from the outside in, you let all the outside garbage in. Let the sun shine from the inside out and all around for others to see. Join right in with all the fun.

By living and being the real me (not pretending who I really am), I am a child of God, and I'm proud of who I am—free to be me; that is where it first began.

Go for it, and dare to be different. Let the showing begin.

Be the real you!

It starts today!

Introduction

Dare to Be You

In life, you think you have it all figured out—how you are going to live your life and how it will be played out. But in turn, God has a different plan that is much better than the one we have for ourselves. It's kind of like he lets us have control for the first half of our lives.

In other words, he give us the reins for a little while to see what we do and see what messes we create—like leaving our children home by themselves for the very first time when we're gone on a long weekend. It's to test us and see what kind of messes we come home to. We have things to face after the dusts settles, and the party's all over and everyone goes home. God brings to our attention what has been going on that we thought we would not have to face. The things we let go for so long was our choice to ignore.

The more you put it off, the angrier you become. It turns into a runaway train with no chance to get off; you're out of control and no chance to grow. It is hard at times to face things you know in your heart need to be done. Doing it yourself, you didn't know quite how to do it, and that's why everything gets so out of control. God will come to the rescue and bring you back to where the story first began.

You can start again. Don't focus on what you did in the past, but take the lessons you learned and move forward. Don't camp out on them, but move on from there. We all have tests and trials we have to go through. The attitude you have while you are going through them determines how long you will stay in them.

Remember it is only a test and what God wants you to learn from this. When you are faced with a trial and burdens, your chosen course of action will determine the results and the outcome. When you go in one way, you come out a better way.

The harder it is, the better the results and the outcome will be. When you are put to the hardest tests, you want to resist. You want to run away from the pain and pretend everything is okay, and life is grand. Soon, reality sets in, and what has been going on inside for so long boils over and oozes over onto everyone else. They have no idea what just happened. It's bound to happen when you don't learn to face things head on when they are first upon you.

One day, rest assured, it will happen that the real you comes out and shines like a diamond in a rough that has been rolling and spinning, being buffeted around, with pieces chipped here and there. Lines drawn are uniquely placed with divine presence where it needs to be. Corners are rounded, smoothing off the razor-rough edges.

Once edges are shaped to be where they need to be, each day the stone is polished and cleaned of dust until it's sparkling, little by little, moment by moment. The light shines through beautiful sparkling colors, through your heart, as the diamond comes to the surface for all to see.

It has been hidden just below the surface for so long, waiting and wanting to come out and shine. The time is now to come out and shine. Why put off until tomorrow what you can do today? Take time to smell flowers today; rain will fall tomorrow. Enjoy the moments you are in. Two days from tomorrow will be today, but the moments of today will be memories of tomorrow. So make the best of today for the brighter tomorrows that are yet to come.

Talk to God and ask him what he sees. It isn't exactly what you see because he sees the real you—what you can be and what you need to be. It is exactly what you need to see—the real you in action. Where you have never been is exactly where you need to be. Listen to your heart. He will lead you where you need to be and show you what you need to do.

Don't just talk about it; do what needs to be done. Don't just wish it was done, but get it done. No more pretending things are getting done when you know full well they are not getting done. The only way to get things done is to put some action behind the plan to achieve the results that you know in your heart you want to see.

Stepping out and letting go will make a world of a difference. Don't be afraid. Dare to be different; that's what's it's all about. You're not here to be like someone else. You're here to be you, not to be something you are not. Be the real you, bold and courageous and confident. That only comes from God. He gives it to you every step of the way. Put your trust in him, and you'll be on your way to being all you can be. Each day get up and thank God for what he has done and for what is yet to come in your life. Talk positively and know each day is brand new.

Step forward. No looking back or going backward. Forward is the best way to go. In the far blue yonder, trust is the only way to get to where you want to go, to reach the dreams that are in store for you. Each step you take and the tests and trials you face as you go through it will bring you to where you need to go.

We all have stepping stones in life. Some are jagged, some are smooth, but we need each and every one of them. From who you once were to where you are right now is exactly where you need to be. Where you are going will lead up to heaven some day.

Down here, we all on a journey. No one gets out of the journey. You might as well enjoy where you are and where you are going. It is in God's hands—the time that all things have taken place. The curves and the rivers we cross, and the mountains we climb, and ponds we wade in, we sink to the bottom, but soon we float back up to the surface, and we go again.

Sometimes we fall and sometimes we trip, but the most important thing is to get up and go again.

The real you takes a stand. Each time you step out and do something out of the ordinary, the bolder you become. You get out of the boat, and you get going, and you are out in the middle before you even know what happened. You need confidence to jump that fence you have been riding for so long. Life's too short to stay there.

Fight the good fight of faith. Action takes away what fear leaves behind with no action. Being fearless is the only way to go. Don't wait another moment. Jump in with both feet. Your feelings will catch up with you. Step out and find out what life's all about. Be a risk taker. You never know what tomorrow may bring.

Accept the opportunity of a lifetime and an adventure that comes by only once. Jump on it, and see where it takes you. Go for it. Life's too short to keep putting it off until tomorrow. You don't know about tomorrow, but you know about today.

Be the real you!
Be the best *you* that you can be.
Share with someone today.

An Overview

Writing this book has taken me on a journey. I didn't know what it entailed or what I would go through until I was in the midst of it. It was hard at first when my true self was starting to arise from the inside. I didn't know what was next or what was around the corner until God knew I was ready to face it. Then it was allowed to come out and slowly work through to get beyond the fear that was holding me back. When you try to run from fear and not deal with it right away, instead coming back to it later, it doesn't work because it will always be there.

God always brings you back to where things go haywire and begins to go wrong and where the hurt first began. It's where you buried the hurt and your true self, but you don't know that until it came back to you in a dream. And you think if you bury it, it's gone for good. But in reality it's never gone unless you release it and let go of it. What is holding you back from showing the real you—the real you that God intended you to be, a bold and confident you?

You are a child of God that he loves and cares for deeply. He loves all his children, indeed he does. Slowly finding out he really does is so freeing; he does love you. When you love yourself as God loves you, you will be able to love others in the same way. God accepts me the way I am, so I can accept me and others too. No more trying to get others to love you if you don't love yourself and accept yourself just the way you are. You won't be able to love others either.

The more you try to be something you're not, and you try to be like someone else thinks you need to be, the more it will not work. In turn, when you compromise to be something you are not, you are trying to fit others into a mold of what you think they ought to be as well.

Let go of that notion and that unrealistic expectation you put on yourself. Don't compromise yourself to get others to like you. It is no good for others, and it's no good for you. You start self-loathing and say, "What is wrong with me? I need to change this or that to get others to like me." No matter what you do, they're still not going to like you. They do for a while, until you do something that they don't approve of, or they are through with you when you're all used up. Then you're dropped when another fool comes along who will do the same thing you just put yourself through. You see they were not your friends at all, not with the things they put you through, the things you did to change for what they needed. They got you to perform for them in the midst of a storm, and it got you nowhere.

Once you step into that arena, things will begin to change, not for the better but for the worst either. You act like something you know you are not. It's like you are on a roller coaster ride, and you're strapped in, ready to go, and you can't get off until the ride is over. When the ride is over, your head and your heart just aches like it is coming out of your chest. And you cry during the ride, going through the turns and curves. Your head feels big as all the air rushes in. And the tears grow worse as the bottom drops out. Your butt hits the seat, and reality sets in. The ride is about at the end, and you are relieved when it's over. You tell yourself, "I am not riding that ride again," but you do it again and again. Each time you compromise yourself again.

You don't realize it until you are buckled in. You say to yourself. "What are you doing? You are on that ride once again." But this time you're on a train. You think this time will be different, but it's like a train wreck waiting to happen. And sooner or later it becomes a train wreck, just like the roller coaster ride. You get hurt in the same way, or it turns out the same. Your heart aches and pain all over again. It's best not to get on that train or that roller coaster one more time because it turns out the same.

By not being yourself, you lose so much. Most of all, you lose your true self. It takes a while to find you once again. And when you do, though, it was worth it. You let the real you out and let yourself shine through and through. Forgive yourself and stop trying to hurt yourself all the time by letting others control you. The fear of rejection is the hardest test of all to pass. Surrender; let it go and walk away.

Writing this book, I learned a lot about me, the real me. Through my journey with God's love and guidance, the truth was revealed to me, one step at a time. I'm where I am today by being free, by letting go of all the things that held me back. I was able to dance freely around for everyone to see the real me, and that's the way it's going to be. Let your hair flow freely in the breeze, through and through. Believe what's in your heart. Go and do what he is telling you to do. And you will achieve what has been burning down deep. Let the love out. Know that the love you have inside is ready to come out in the words you speak.

Dare to be yourself. The real you will come out and shine if you allow it to do so. Step out, and be all you want to be. Who cares what others think? This is you. If you don't like it, it's your problem, not mine. I don't need your approval to live my life the way I want to. Everyone has a unique and divine quality to them and a plan as well.

Accept yourself the way you are, and you will accept others as well. Let go of all the past hurts, and get past of what others think of you. Do what's in your heart. Don't let yourself down. If you do, you will start sinking back into your quicksand, and soon you'll want to disappear. Stand clear; that isn't the answer at all. You need to stand up and say, "No. This it's not for me. It might be okay for you but not for me."

Be yourself and have fun and enjoy your day. Others might not be cheering you on when you run your own race, but God is. Step forward and take hold of his hand; that is the best advice to running your race and things you need to face.

Dare to love yourself; that's the best test of all. Doing so is the best gift you can give yourself. The love and the words spoken will encourage others and you. Don't let others still your joy and the dreams you sought. Go for it! God has a great plan for you and me.

CHAPTER 1

Pretend

You say everything is okay
When it is far from being correct; you are a wreck.
You say yes when everything inside is screaming no.
You're pretending you're okay when you know you are not.
You say you can pay for something when you know you cannot.
You say yes because you think that's what they want to hear.
Instead, it makes it worse when you don't face what you need to.
Holding onto something that needs to be put to
rest; and letting it go so you can grow.
By pretending you're something when you are not, just to fit in.
When you compromise you will have to keep it up.
It keeps getting bigger over time, until you are out of control.
Stop and let go.
Start again.
Move forward and don't look back on what lies behind you.
Look at what the future has in store for you.
Each day is brighter and lighter than you ever thought possible.
Stand up and take about-face.
The future awaits you.
It's a new beginning.
Yesterday ended last night.
Today is a brand-new morning.
When you feel like you are going backward, don't go there.

Keep your eyes focused on what lies ahead.
Not what others are doing; it is none of your business.
Concentrate on what you are doing.
Who cares what others think you should or shouldn't be doing?
Do what you need to do, not just say this needs to be done.
Take action; that's the only way it will get done.
Wishing it will get done, it will never get done.
It only makes it worse as the time goes by.
Face it now, or face it later.
Someday you will have to face it.
Face it, and get on with it; that's the only way to get through it.
It will take discipline to get it done.
You can do it; make up your mind, and you'll get it done.
With hard work and determination, you will make it through
To the other side; you will see
The real you and me, no more pretending.
The truth is the only way to get things done.
What is done is done, and what needs to be
done will be done when it gets done.
Have fun as you're getting things done.
Enjoy all the things that are done along the way
With the ones you love as you see the way to the other side.
All the sunsets and rainstorms you run through,
the clouds overhead take you forth.
A new-day adventure just above the horizon awaits you.
Stop pretending; that's blinding you.
Get to living; you don't want to miss a thing.
Be the real you.

CHAPTER 2

The Unrealistic Perfection

When God put a mirror in front of me, it showed me what had been going on. I knew in my heart there was something going on, but I couldn't understand what it was. Now, it slowly comes to mind. For years I experienced self-loathing because I thought everything needed to be perfect to be right. To be perfect was unrealistic in an imperfect world. That's no life at all.

I put so much pressure on myself to be perfect and right all the time that it broke my heart, and I lost myself in the process. In fact, in God's eyes being right some of the time is just right. Not having the lines right, the divine is perfectly right.

When you let go of unrealistic perfection, better things begin to flow together. You will see life in a different light altogether. Your heart will see what your eyes don't by the way you view things that are going on around you.

Life is divinely designed with each one of us in mind.

When you put yourself on a pedestal that you cannot maintain, it puts you out of sorts. The best thing that can happen is it hurts at first when you come tumbling down. The pressure is released when you let go of all that nonsense you have been putting yourself through. The meaning of being perfect is letting go of being perfect. Then it's divinely perfect, the way it is to be. Being open and honest is the best way to surpass and let go of the past.

It is what it is; I am who I am and I don't need to be like someone else to be me. To compare myself with someone else is nonsense.

God made us all to be different, so we can help to bring out the best in each other, instead of trying to beat and bash each other, trying to outdo each other.

It makes no sense.

We all do it some way or another, trying to be someone we're not, trying to fit into something we shouldn't be in. In the first place, it hurts and cuts down deep, more than you know, when you don't accept yourself for who you are, by the words you say, and the things you do. Your actions are heavy, and your words are strong, with power behind them.

So choose your words wisely. You can make or break someone with one word or one phrase spoken. Encourage and engage someone to go for his or her dreams; don't stand in the way. Even in the midst of the stream, the words will go farther and reach them. The heart will grow sounder, and the light is there. We need to take notice.

A spark can spread like a wildfire to bring joy to the air and a light to a heart that once was dark and cold as steel.

Now it is as warm as a summer sunset in the
Colorado Rockies skies—beautiful as ever.

When you share the love that's in your heart, it reaches down deep like nothing before could touch. That is love, and it's so amazing. What a transformation right in front of your eyes by reaching out and loving someone back. It changes both hearts in the process, right from the start. With no rules set in place, you feel peace when you get to be your true self. The joy comes back; it fills up the air all around you. You begin to let the walls down, and slowly your heart opens as love enters. No more hiding your pain as the rain sets in. Tears trickle down your cheeks and wash all the blemishes away. The spots in our hearts are made clean; we get to begin again.

The brokenness is slowly brought around, and the pieces are moved into new spots in our hearts. A new chapter has started as you begin to move forward, and the plan has been set forth for you to go onward. Don't question yesterday. It's a day from which to learn and grow. To reach your new destination is to look forward and not live in the past. The past is the past, and that is where it will always be. There is no reverse and no do-overs. Keep looking ahead and not in your rear view mirror.

The future is ahead of you, and the adventures and the journey through the new chapters are yet to follow. Don't write off your future by what happened in the past or what is going on in the present. Each new day is an adventure of itself. Look forward to the horizon. What's up ahead it is so broad, and it's waiting for you. Take that leap of faith, and go for your dreams that God has in bestowed in your heart.

We all have a dream or a vision of how we see the future, of where we'll be years down the road. Keep your dreams alive with each step you take. If you lost your dream that you once had envisioned, it's time to dust off your heart and begin again.

Start anew, and open your heart to let in the love.

Everything changes, and nothing stays the same. I'm so glad that God likes to change things up. Can you imagine how boring life would be if everything stayed the same? Day in and day out, all of us would be like robots going around in circles. The next day would be the same as it was the day before and the day before that. It sounds boring to keep doing the same thing as everyone else is doing.

I'm so glad that God doesn't let us know what's ahead of us. It's better to trust God in everything, and keep our faith alive. If we didn't, we probably would go crazy trying to figure out the master plan. Since that's not going to happen, trying to figure everything out, it's best to leave it alone. Leave it in God's hands, and trust he has everything under control with his master plan. Even when things happen and we don't understand why; remember there is a reason, but we don't need to know.

I believe and trust you, even when I don't understand.

"Trust in the Lord with all your heart and lean not on your own understanding" (Proverbs 3:5).

Even when our hearts get broken—and sometimes they do—he will help us through. Keep moving forward, and hold your head up high, even when things don't go your way. Help and encourage someone who has lost his or her way, so that person will begin to see the light once again. Share what's in your heart; it's a delight, and the light is shining bright in your heart tonight. Life is what you make of it and the attitude you take when things come your way.

God throws curves your way and tests you.
The trials you face are there to help you, not hurt you.

It helps us to become stronger as we live longer and enables us to stand. Don't let things bother you as they once did. In this way, before the tests and trials and the curves and the bumps in the road, we learn over time and go with what life throws at us. It helps us not to run away. There is something for us to learn from each and every experience in our journeys. are

Keep believing and moving forward, and take the lemons you are given and turn them into lemonade—and share with others. Life is a gift you were given; enjoy every moment. No more living with the unrealistic expectations you've put on yourself and others. Live your life, and share all the colors of love. You will touch someone's life through yours by the way you live your life out loud.

Love is shown each step you take.

How fun that will be to see you—the real you in full bloom!

CHAPTER 3

Brand-New Day

As you wake up, you look at the sky, and the sun begins to warm your face. Now the storm has passed. It's like a long time has passed as each day passes. For each moment you have in your life, lots and lots of tests and trials shape you to be what you are to be. For each thing you go through, remember: this too shall pass. There is something you are to learn and take with you, onward, down the road.

Today is a *brand-new day* for you to enjoy. Each day is a gift; rejoice in this day the Lord has made just for you and me.

Today is your day; nothing can stand in your way. Go ahead and do your best with no regrets. Have fun writing your own story, day by day, moment by moment. Believe in your dreams. They will come true. Just wait and see all the plans that have been put into place.

Your heart will speak to you if you truly listen and don't turn away. Today is a brand-new day to spread your wings and fly, even when life throws you curve. Your life may fall apart for a little while, but in due time, the pieces will start to fall back into place once again.

Although you never thought it possible, you'll have joy once again. You will see the smile form on your face. You'll feel joy when you help others begin to heal by the words you speak. You've been in their shoes, and the steps you have taken were also taken by the ones before these days.

The brand-new day—you have it to enjoy, even when you have no joy to speak of. By getting up and get going again, it shows you have hope. Others see what you do and see that what you say is true by the feelings you share. It's what you have been through and what you go through day after day when a loved one goes home. You still feel the pain after the days have passed.

It doesn't go away like the flip of a hat and—snap—the pain goes away. You'll never want to feel that pain again after time goes by. It doesn't stay on the surface like before, but it goes into another part of your heart—the soft part of your heart that is under lock and key.

You know it is there each morning when you awake and when you go to sleep at night. It feels like something is still missing, and you'll always ache, even when you're awake. From the inside out, you know in your heart that you will see that person once again, but it still doesn't make it any easier. Time goes on, and you learn to tolerate the pain and the way of doing things differently in your life. Know that there is a new road laid out for you, a rough road ahead with the new surface you're on.

No turning back the wheels of time. Wheels only move forward. The reality sets in that this is real, and the person is not coming back, not even when you think, *If only I had done this or that, he would be here.*

Life is but a journey that we are all on, and some of us go home earlier than others. The ones who are left to carry on know it takes a lot of strength and determination to go on without those who are gone. In your heart, God shows you it will be okay. Even when you don't think you can take another step, each day is a brand-new day to carry on.

To get up and go another day without that someone is hard, but it will be okay as time goes by. It's another day and another week. Soon it will be a month and then a year without that person here.

You'll have ups and downs and rocky and wavy moments in your day. You'll have sunshine in the midst of the rain. It seems like yesterday that person went away, but in your heart it seems like today.

On a brand-new day, God gives you love and comfort to help you through. He puts up distractions to take your mind off what you have been thinking about all the day long, now that your special someone is gone. He or she will never be forgotten; that person will always have a special place in your heart. As time goes by, the darkest part in your heart is now a lighter blue, with a few clouds floating around from time to time. A bit of sunshine you thought you would never see again slowly starts to peek over your shoulder as you move forward.

You feel the warmth on your face that you once felt, cold from all the tears you've cried. The tears that you cry heal you from the inside out, as you begin to shout. No one knows how long it takes to get going on your way to a brand-new way of living, but you and your heart will take as long as it takes. Don't rush the grief you feel. It has to take its time to heal. It's not an overnight deal, as others might think, as it is when they get over losing a pet, or a neighbor moving away, or losing a tooth; it doesn't quite work that way.

It cuts down deep into your soul, like nothing you have ever felt or ever experienced before, that day.

Don't get me wrong; grief is still grief. Until you lose a child that pain is like no other pain you could have ever encountered. So when people say they understand, they couldn't possible understand until they have put on your shoes on and walked in them for a while. Then they possible could understand what you are going through.

I'm getting this off my chest to let others know what's going on, how a heart can break into a million pieces right in front of you. No one even knows it unless you express it once and for all. Instead of explaining everything you are feeling and saying why you are acting this way, people have to be told, "No, I don't want to hurry up and get over my heartache." It's because it makes them uncomfortable, and they don't know what to say, when they see the hurt and pain on your face. So they take the easy way out and don't come around. Maybe that's better that way. It makes you stronger as you lean on God; he's our provider, and it brings you closer to him. It's okay if you feel that way. God always brings new friends your way, as the old ones slowly fade away.

It's not good to bottle up everything. When you do, sooner or later you'll want to explode. It's like opening a wound that has puss, and you cut it open, and it sprays all over. With one big explosion, that's all it takes to get all the poison out of you. The best thing to do is to let it all out, once and for all, so the real healing can begin. Your tears come down like rain and start washing the walls of your heart and soul. It's like a cleaning from the inside out, slowly healing and picking up the pieces and arranging them all about in all sorts of fashion. By letting go, you'll really be able to go forward instead of holding on to the past and living real fast.

It's time to let go of all the hurt that you
need to lay to rest once and for all.

When all the hurt is brought to the surface, letting it go is the best medicine you can take. It takes courage to let go of all the hurt you are feeling. To go forward, it is best to keep looking ahead and not live in the past; you'll have no rest. If you keep going backward and hit the dust, all you'll want to do is rust as you hit the ground and you bust. Let it go; it's for the best.

Today is a *brand-new day* to begin again. Everything has changed; nothing stays the same. We all get a chance to begin again. Life throws you curves and delays that take you off track for a while. As one chapter ends, a new one begins. No reason to watch reruns of your life. It's a new life and a new story to tell. Finish the one that has started; it has come full circle. Add new chapters and new characters you meet along the road of discovering *you* again. Walk along the road of where you've been and move on to where you are going.

Today is a brand-new day to enjoy what's ahead, and let go of what lies behind. As you open your heart for all the love others want to give you; you will be able to give too. Take your time; there's no rush. Slow down and enjoy your brand-new day in a brand-new way.

Have fun and let your hair down. Run through the rain as you did as a young child. Do and try new things that put a smile on your face.

Today is a brand-new day!
Enjoy the brand-new you!

CHAPTER 4

Notes from Above

Let me guide you, and peace will return.
Take a look and review.
Your way—there is no peace in your heart.
My way—peace will fill your heart.
Listen to your heart.
Believe what you hear.
Let go of your chains.
Trust me; I will not let you fail.
I will hold your hand all the way.
When you slip and fall, look up.
I will be there to lift you up.
I will be there to put your feet on the ground.
It's your choice;
Your choice to make, no one else s.
Make a positive decision today.
Don't go around that same mountain.
Make positive changes.
Honor God with your hopes and dreams.
Also with your everyday life.
Look and see.
Your way.
God's way.
You will receive more

Than you can ever imagine.
Take that first step.
You will be glad you did.
Think about it.
Staying the same makes no difference; you
stay in one spot and go nowhere.
Staying the same is hard and remains harder and harder as you go.
In addition, you get the same results that you started out with.
Nowhere.
Keep remembering change can make a difference as you go farther.
Dream big, and reach your destiny.
Change—it starts out hard, but it becomes
easier and easier as you go.
You will reach what you set out to do by not giving up.
By determination and pressing onward.
Dream big!

CHAPTER 5

Believe What's in Your Heart

The day comes in your life when you believe
what you can see or what you can't see.

Your heart says one thing, but you see things in a different way. What do you do and say when you feel this way? You know what's in your heart is right. It has never steered you wrong before; why would it start now?

Keep believing and move forward; its only way to go. It is there to guide you the right way and steer you down the narrow path God has laid out for you.

Believe with your whole heart that's where true faith and love begins, when you step out and grab hold of his hand to guide you through the darkness and the unknown. You know it is going to be great when you get there. It will be a little rocky at first and with each step you take.

It will be worth every step you take.

Believe and walk by faith and not by sight. Trust each and every day and depend on God; he does have your best interest in mind. What you believe will come out in what you say and do. Why not put your full trust in God? You have nothing to worry about. He has all your bases covered. God loves you so much, and he is capable of taking care of all your needs.

Love endures all possible ways. Open your heart and find out. Your journey ahead is awesome. You'll see more from your heart than you ever did before. What is holding you back from being the real you? The first steps are once you really let go and start believing. Be the real you and not a version of what someone else thinks you should be.

God made us unique in every way possible. Spread your wings and fly; live from the inside out. Start believing and put your trust in God. He knows what he is doing, even when you do not. You've driven long enough. Time to let go and let God take over in the driver's seat.

Really put your trust in him and know
your breakthrough is coming.

Turn things around, and you'll be able to see life in a different light. All you need to do is open your heart and believe from the inside out. Live out loud, laugh often, and cry when you need to. Have a willing heart to help others, and dance when others aren't watching.

Love with all your heart; be kind to others, even when they are not kind to you.

Be there for others when their hearts are broken.
Shed some light all around in a dark place.
The time is now to be the real you.
If you long to make a difference, you will
stand out by being the real you.
Be all that you can be.
What God intended for you, so long ago, is
to be unique in every way possible.
Live out loud and have fun along the way.
Encourage others to do the same, to reach for their dreams as well.
They're for all of us to reach.
Enjoy others as themselves, and live out loud, laugh, and have fun.

Share what's in your heart and believe
what's down deep in your heart.
Be a light in a dark place; once you start
It won't be long, and the dark will begin to turn.

Share your light, the bright light that is
burning in your heart tonight!

Believe it is all you need to do, and keep your hope
alive, and your dreams will be on their way.
Press on! Forward!

Reach for the stars, and take a leap of faith as you do.
You might land on the moon and get all
that you hoped for, and more,
Just by believing and trusting, dreaming, and loving along the way.
Treat others as you would like to be treated.

Believe … what's in your heart from the start.

You will never go wrong. As long as you have love and peace to
go around, you'll have joy. So before you make a drastic decision,
see if you have peace do it. If you don't have peace, don't do it.

Believe … do what's in your heart.
You can't go wrong!

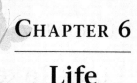

CHAPTER 6

Life

Where are you?
Are you watching the game?
Are you on the bench?
You're taking a time out for too long; don't sit on the bench
until the time runs out; get in the game. Show what you are
made of and play; you see your team losing the game.
It's time to jump in and help change the game
So we all win! The game!
Encourage others to get into the game to win too! Everyone wins!
When we are all in the game to play, we have fun.
Enjoy our game of life together.
It is more fun when you encourage others.
We all fall down, and get up again. Play the game; we all win!

CHAPTER 7

To Live Out Loud Takes Courage

Everything changes; nothing stays the same.
Step out in faith, and see what's on the other side.

Watching from the sidelines, everything stays the same, as the world keeps going around and around. Nothing stays the same when you get back in the game of life. You've sat long enough; it's time to step up and get moving again. Dream again; you'll find out and see where it takes you.

To live out loud takes courage.

Be aggressive and determined to never give up on your dreams or whatever you set out to do. No more hiding your true self; be all you can be. When you feel a bit overwhelmed, and you don't know where to turn, take a moment and give yourself a time-out.

Stretch arms, shut your eyes for a moment, and take a deep breath and relax. A sense of peace will wrap around your body, which leaves you comfort and joy. It always looks better than it did before you took your time-out.

Be bold and live out loud.

It takes courage to live a dream and live it out loud. Each step you take is a little bit closer to seeing your dream. As you go onward, face your fears that arise, and see your dream come true, you're one step closer. Keep it in your heart; you're almost there; keep going. Don't give up now. It's just above the horizon; you can almost touch it. It's beyond the river and over the hill; you can almost see it and smell the flowers in the valley.

If you give up in the middle of the stream, you'll miss out on the robins singing in the valley. By not giving up on dreams, we sit by the streams and remember that everyone falls down sometimes. Getting back up is the best choice you can make.

When you trip and fall, you're not giving up; you're warming up. You hear that voice—*you can do it; get up and go again. You're almost there.* The game isn't over yet; you have many miles to go. Face your fears. Do it afraid if you have to. You can do it; put your mind to it. You have what it takes. Remember fear arises when you have the most to gain. That's when we also have the most to lose. That's when your faith comes in, and the truth prevails.

Take that risk. Be a risk taker or a wish maker, and go no farther than that. A wish is a dream waiting to come true. You need backbone, not wishbone, to reach your dreams.

Until you have action behind your dream, it won't go any further. You have what it takes; it's a brand-new day. *Go for it* and *live out loud.* It takes hope and faith and a lot of hard work and determination to make it work.

It takes courage not to listen to naysayers and the Negative Nellies saying, "This will never happen. You can't do this, and you can't do that." Just know when people say it, that's because they don't have the courage to live out loud themselves. Until they do, they will never be happy. Who cares what others think? Start living out loud; you will be glad you did.

The love in your heart doesn't just sit there; it gets going again. Each day is a brand-new day to get up and shine. This day was made just for you to spread your wings and *live out loud.*

You need to do what you love and love what you do, and touch lives along the way. Make it a little brighter for someone who passes your way. It takes courage to live this way, the right way.

What's truly in your heart that's keeping you still? *Live out loud* with colors flowing out of you; face your fear. Face it here and now. The sooner you do, the sooner you will be able to live your true colors out loud.

Take the first step and face what you need to face.
The courage that's down deep, you can do it.
God is with you every step of the way.
What do you need to face?
Once you face it, you'll be able to face another and another.

Each time it gets a little easier, and you get a little stronger on each road you face. Be determined to make things happen. Don't wish for them to happen. Keep your focus; any little distraction keeps you from action.

When you get distracted and feelings of throwing in the towel start to arise, say, "No, I'm not going there." You've come too far to give up now. I'm doing what I'm supposed to be doing. If you don't like it, it's not my problem. I'm doing what God is telling me to do, not what others are telling me to do. I'm living what I know, not how I feel any longer.

When you *live out loud* you will feel more alive than you have in years. That's the way it's going to be from now on. Live out loud, and let go, and let your hair down, and don't live so uptight when things don't go right. The more fears you begin to face, the more you run your own race, instead of letting others run your race for you. We all have dreams and fears to face. So face your fears that are holding you back from reaching your dreams. Go for it, and take a risk, and start *living out loud*, and keep your dreams alive.

What are you afraid of—making it, or regretting, hurting, and making mistakes and letting others down? No one is going to hurt you unless you allow others to continue to use you, control you, and manipulate you to do what they want you to do.

Whatever it may be, letting yourself down is the biggest regret of all. Compromise to fit in. You will never fit in. No matter what you do, it will never work.

No more, it's time to take a stand, to face
your fears throughout the years.
Letting go is the first step to moving on.
When you face your fears, you get past
what's really holding you back.
You're able to face anything life throws your way.

Go for it, and let it go, and be all you can be.
All you have to do is believe in yourself, be
true to yourself, and love yourself.
Respect yourself, and *live out loud*, and dance when you hear music.

Be yourself; you don't need others' approval.
You have God, and that's all you need to be you.
That's all any of us needs.
To be free, God's the key to unlock the door to *live out loud*.

God is smiling down on you and me.
Go for it; take that step.
It takes courage to *live out loud*.

CHAPTER 8

Things to Ponder—
Peaceful Easy Living

How do you perceive yourself? Is it how you perceive others? Everything you perceive about yourself is what you will perceive everything else to be. Sit back and take a look in the mirror. As you look over your life so far, you will learn so much. Things slowly will be revealed to you as you ponder things played about in your memory.

It starts to make better sense why things are going the way they are going. Things begin to unfold as you ponder things in your mind. You will see sights and examples of the different thoughts you have about yourself. Once you change your outlook on yourself, it will change your whole life's outlook as well.

- How you perceive yourself is how you will perceive others.

Example: If you don't believe in yourself, you won't believe in others. When you begin to believe in yourself, others will believe in you too.

- How you see yourself is how you will see others.

Example: You see your flaws, and you see everyone's flaws as well.

- How you talk about yourself is how you talk about others.

Example: When you comment about your flaws, you will also comment about someone else.

- How you compare yourself to others is how you compare others to you.

Example: You wish you could be someone else; you compare that person to you.

- You compare what you wear to what others are wearing.

Example: You don't think what you are wearing is good enough. You compare others' clothing to what you are wearing, or you make fun of it, or you want what they have, especially when someone comments about your outfit, good or bad, whatever it may be.

- You try to impress people, but you only hurt others as well as yourself.

Example: When you try to impress others, you are like a puppet on a string. Once you bow down, it's a losing battle. The only one who is going to get hurt in the process is you, by not being you. Anyone who wants to change the real you only wants something from you. In other words, others use you for personal gain and never liked you from the beginning.

So the harder you try to impress and the more you try to fit in, the less likely it is that you will fit in, no matter how hard you try. All the fires you put out will never be good enough. The more you try, the worse things seem to get. Don't try to change into something that you aren't meant to be. As soon you realize that, you become more of a people pleaser to fit in. It only leads to disaster.

The worse you view others, the more you begin to despise yourself. You think there is something really wrong. With the wrong mind-set, you think you need to do more and more and then they will like you more. *Wrong!* Because the more you do, the more you tell yourself that you will be *never good enough*. Now you have sold yourself out, and your heart is breaking.

That's exactly how you will talk to yourself and to others. No matter what they do or you do, it will never be good enough. You try to make everything perfect, but you'll drive yourself crazy trying to perform and keep others happy; it will be at your expense. It will never be good enough, no matter what you do. They will never be happy, and you will only be sad, and soon you will get mad.

Whatever you did will never be enough. That's why everyone needs to be in charge of their own happiness. That way, they'll only have one person to blame as they look in the mirror, not those around them or the circumstances around them. It's hard to please the unpleasing. It is a vicious circle as you please others all the time, and in turn you expect others to please you. It costs you so much more; the one who usually pays for it is you.

- You listen to others say things, and you try to make everything perfect.

In other words, you upset the apple cart to keep the peace. There's always a fight by always being right. You make yourself miserable by trying to keep everyone happy. Your heart is breaking from the inside out. You lie to yourself when you try to keep everything perfect all around you. It's a never-ending battle from the inside out. It's a mountain you cannot climb, but mountains you keep going around and around, like a ride spinning out of control.

That's no life at all. Sit up and take notice. The time is now to make a change, and put your trust in God. Let go of always trying to please everyone.

Once you let go, the healing will begin. God is your guide. He will see you through to the other side of your pain. Look above; how you perceive yourself can affect your whole life.

Take a moment and think of yourself. You know in your heart it isn't right, and a tear is near. Your heart needs a hug from above. Ask God to help you to forgive and make peace with yourself. God will show you what is wrong, but in turn, he helps make everything right, even when you make mistakes and your thinking is all wrong; even when you think nothing can go wrong and that everything needs to be perfect.

The more you try, the more turmoil you bring on yourself, which brings on more pain. That hurts you down deep in your soul, and your heart grieves for you. You don't know your heart is slowly breaking, quietly inside, when you compromise or sell yourself out to fit in.

Then you take on the role that you don't need anybody, but, in fact, everyone needs somebody sometimes. That's why God has placed everyone with different talents and gifts to help each other along the way. It's okay to make mistakes. That's how we learn and grow, by the mistakes we make. God made it that way so we will need him every step of the way. We're nothing without God and his guidance in our lives.

Think about it: if everything was perfect, we wouldn't need God for anything. That's the wrong way of thinking because that's the way the world thinks. Right now, with there are selfish intentions, where you need to do everything yourself to get what you want, no matter who you hurt in the process. But who you really hurt is yourself in the long run. Then when you don't get your way, you start the blaming and complaining game.

That happens when you try to be perfect all the time. It's not your job to fix things that cannot be fixed, that only God can fix. You didn't know you were trying to take over God's job or someone else's responsibility, who tried to pass it on to someone else to fix.

When things don't work out quite as you planned or the way you think it should have been done, you get mad at yourself and say hurtful things to yourself. As you do, you begin to take it out on others, and you spew angry, ugly words all over them.

By jumping in and taking over to make everything perfect, nothing will go right.You will hurt yourself and others around you by doing something you had no business doing in the first place. In the long run, trying to be perfect and keeping everyone happy in perfect harmony will never work. Nothing is perfect in an imperfect world.

Jesus has paved the road for all of us to be free to be ourselves. Jesus died for all of us to live and have an intimate relationship with God. It's time to let go of the notion that if your surrounds are perfect, everything else will be too. Enjoy the journey you're on.

Let everyone be in charge of their own happiness and business. It's not your job to keep everyone happy and beat yourself up in the process by doing it. We all have our own responsibilities. Believe that God is the fixer of all things. Trust that he will fix things in no time flat.

We learn by Jesus's example. He showed love for all of us, and we should live by his example—doing good and loving and accepting others as they are, as well as yourself.

Serve and help others, but don't go overboard by taking over their lives. Live the Word of God out loud, and be a blessing to others along the way. Love with all of your heart. Love everyone as you love yourself—but you can't do that if you don't love yourself. You can't give something away that you don't have to give.

Think: do you love yourself?

If the answer is no, then how can you expect to love others? Your whole being and how you view everything comes down to you—how you treat yourself, how you like yourself, how you talk to yourself, how you love yourself, how you view yourself, how you accept yourself, just as you are, by not trying to be something you're not.

Think about it: the more you try to be something you are not, the worse it gets, and the worse you feel. A heartache begins to show as it comes to the surface.

It's not you, and you are way off base, and you don't like what you've become. You are hurting God and yourself and others in return by not being yourself. You are missing out on so much.

It is important to be yourself and accept yourself the way you are.

God intended for you to be special in every way. God accepts you as you are. Why don't you? He knew exactly what he was getting when he made you.

Accept yourself just the way you are.
Change comes when you accept yourself.

That's the first step.

As you accept yourself, you will begin to accept others as they are, just as Jesus did for you. It's okay to make a mistake; that's how you learn, and you let go and grow from them. You don't have to camp out over them and punish yourself over the mistake you've made. Let it go, and move on. It will be okay in the long run. You can't go back and change yesterday, but you can take what you learned from yesterday.

Go out each day and do your best; that's all God asks. Mistakes come, and you trip and fall over things you did wrong. You knew it was a mistake, and you fall short of your best. Repent and ask for forgiveness—that's all you need to do—and then move on. It's up to you and your choice to make. Give your best; that is all he asks from all of us.

You need God in everything. You are nowhere without him.

The second step

Be yourself, just as God made you. Once you do, you will see where it takes you. The real you will shine through by being you.

Be yourself, and let your unique and divine self shine on others. Show others that they can be themselves, and everything will work out just fine.

No one needs to walk on eggshells due to fear that you're going to offend the other person. Some are afraid that their pain will show up when they do. So they hide behind their pain, thinking it will go away, but it won't if you keep wearing it on your sleeve. The only way to get rid of it is to let it go, and shake off the old pain-filled sleeves. You have been shaking them all about, like salt and pepper shakers that have lost their entire flavor.

It is time to let go and wipe the slate clean. Begin again, and start a new flavor of things. Do something to spice up your life, and try something new and adventurous. Do things that are so out of the norm for you, something that you've always wanted to do, that you once were too afraid to do. The time is now; today is a brand-new day. Stir up your life, and make a decision to do what it takes to begin again.

Your life really begins when you start living from the inside out.
Don't let anything stand in your way.
Today is your day to let your shine out.

The third step and the most important one

Love and respect yourself; it goes hand in hand.
Because when you truly love yourself, you will respect yourself.
God loves you just as you are.
Why not love yourself as God loves you?
You love God, and he made you.

Everything he has made is good, and that includes you. Don't listen to the negative talk about you. Listen to God; he says that you are loved, and you are the apple of his eye.

When you love yourself and others, you honor God at the same time. Let your walls of conditions come down. Let the love in, and you will begin to love yourself and others in the same loving way. Be able to respect yourself enough to say, "I don't have to be perfect to be loved. No more pretending everything is perfect."

No one can escape life without having flaws. It's how you learn and grow. Accept them and move on from them; don't camp out on them. It is a unique part of you. The quirks you have don't explain the way you are. You're free to be you. It's not the end of the world when you make a mistake. Don't make such a big deal out of it or be so hard on yourself. Others make mistakes as well.

When milk gets spilled, it happens; it can't climb back into the glass as if it didn't happen. You deal with it, clean it up, and move on as if it never happened, without pitching a fit every time something happens.

Doing so hurts more and cuts down deep into your soul. Words and actions hurt more than you know if it is handled incorrectly. You know how it makes you feel when someone yells at you for the milk you've spilled. That's how others feel when it happens to them. So hold your tongue and clean up the spilled milk on the floor. Remember we all make mistakes. Ask for forgiveness when you hurt someone.

Forgive and forget

Onto the next adventure of the day—spread love and joy all around. Love covers all things. It isn't the end of the world when you make a mistake.

Let yourself off the hook. Forgive yourself for your past mistakes. Once you do, you will release a sense of peace. When you forgive yourself, it will make it easier to forgive others who have hurt you. When you forgive yourself, you will have gone over one of the biggest hurdles. In the way God has forgiven you, you will be able to forgive others. Receive and accept his forgiveness.

Do you believe in God? Yes, do you believe in Jesus? Yes, do you believe in you? If the answer is no, why not? God believes in you; you should too. He made you, and he knows all about you and loves you.

If you don't believe in yourself, you won't believe in others either. The more you get in agreement and believe what God is telling you, the more you'll start believing in yourself, and the more confidence you'll have in yourself. Carry yourself and talk positively about yourself.

How you treat others is how you treat yourself. When you treat yourself right, you will treat others right. In a positive way, when you treat yourself as God treats you, you will start to blossom into a beautiful flower. You'll be like a ray of sunshine that has a special glow all around. By treating yourself right and others right, blessings will follow.

Focus more on what God wants and less on what others want. When you listen to your heart a little more, the better you'll be. God really wants to help you—not to destroy you but to love you. God has a special plan for your life. Listen more to what God says about you and less what others say about you. What is in your heart? Are you doing exactly what you are supposed to be doing?

Who cares what others are doing? We all have our own rows to hoe. We all have our own races to run. No one will run it for you. Begin to run your race with God; it's an adventure of a lifetime with no regrets. You will never be bored or ever alone. He is with you every step of the way home.

Only listen to the positive about you, and let go of the negative; it will only bring you down. Who cares what others think of you? That's between them and God.

Step out and do something out of the normal realm that's bold and courageous and full of life. The real you will appear. Don't hide in the rear, full of fear. Go for it. You have what it takes to not hide the real you.

Dance and be joyful all day long, and be a blessing to everyone who passes your way. Don't change the real you to make someone else happy. It will never work. Stand straight, and do the best you can. Get up when you fall. Lend a helping hand when others fall down. Encourage others to seek their dreams and reach for the stars that are in their hearts.

All things are possible with God on your side. All you need to do is invite him into your heart, and he will come into your life. Let the big adventure begin, make it all about him, and he will make it all about you. Don't run your life and make it all about you. We know how far that has gotten us. It's time to begin and invite Jesus in. He will be with you every step of the way.

Be yourself, the real you. That's when your life really begins. God made us to do the best we can, and he will take care of the rest. Do your best; that's all he asks. Be all you can be. Love as God loves. It is all about him. God will take care of you.

Every need indeed, sow a seed, and watch
and see the blessings you'll receive.
Be the real you, and I will be the real me.
A peaceful, easy living you will be living. The *real you* will be seen!

CHAPTER 9

Puppet Strings

Are you tired of being a puppet on a string, always going somewhere and getting nowhere? It was too good to last for others to do it for you. What good is it when you don't learn a thing?

The time is here to cut the puppet strings so you can stand on your own two feet. We all do that; the only way to grow and learn is by cutting these strings that are holding you up. At first it will be tough and a little rough to see right now, but in time everything will come to pass, as your feet become firmly planted on the ground.

As you begin the journey to be the bold and confident person we all know and love, start with the knowledge you had at age eighteen—with no fear. You had it all figured out, and the world was in the palm of your hands. We all start out that way. It's the best place to start to review all the things that have taken place.

Your parents talked to you, and you just stared at the walls and tuned them out. You know it all and built a wall of "I know it all, and they know nothing at all." No one was going to tell you how to live or where you were going. They forgot they were kids once too. We had to learn the hard way as well; that's the only way to get through that "I know it all" wall. In turn, we realized we knew nothing at all.

It took a terrible fall before we could see our parents were smart after all. Your parents love you and let you experience things you didn't understand until you were standing on solid ground. Then you could see.

They let the strings go and let you get started to go for your dreams. That will take you places, and you will see the plans God has in store for you. It's time to grow up and soar, and you learn as you go. We can always learn something new. There is a brighter tomorrow by the lessons we learn today.

Go for it; don't let fear stand in your way because of what happened yesterday. God will be with you every step of the way to help you see your brighter tomorrow and reach the dreams you had as a child. Things happen to you and to me, but it will work out in the end. It's time to begin; your future awaits you and your destiny needs you. Others cannot make decisions for you or live your life for you. The choices are yours to make. Start living out your dreams, and see where it takes you. What's on the screen? What you envision it to be, it will be. Live what's in your heart—see it, believe it, and receive it.

Have faith. All your dreams will come true. No more walls to hide the real you. Shine and be the real you, and your dreams will come true. All you need to do is believe, even when you fall down. Get up and go again. No more pretending; it's come to an end. No more fear; there may be tears, but don't hold back. March through and keep climbing until the end, even when the strings are stretched wide open.

Be a bold and confident person.

CHAPTER 10

Selfish and Mean

When others are selfish and mean, that doesn't mean you have to see what you can be by being selfish and mean. It doesn't work that way. Think the best, even when others act the worst. They will always be selfish and mean if they chose to be. That doesn't mean that you have to be. They have to be willing to change; you can't do it for them. The choice is theirs to make. If you make it easy, it won't happen. Sometimes the best but hardest medicine is to walk away. Bless them and release them. That's when you will see a change. It's when your faith and trust are put to the test, when you have the most to gain and the most to lose.

Life is too short to live in knots around someone who is selfish and mean. They only want to bring you down and lift themselves up to cover the hurt with all the dirt that's on their shirt. They steal your joy and leave you sad, and then they're glad to leave you sad by being selfish and mean. Someone did it to them and left them this way. Hearts left unspoken is a token of hearts broken. It's sad to see someone selfish and mean get what you need.

Be kind and loving to those who are not nice. They will begin to think twice as they throw their dice and start being nice by you being nice. The picture will slowly change into a different frame of mind and bring out the colors that haven't been seen by the one being mean. It only takes one to bring out the best of another and breaks the shell that's covered by the pain that was caused by another. Find out the why, and you will find the root of the whole picture. Look inside the heart as everything begins to melt, and before long the light will come on.

It always comes around to benefit both involved. Spread the love in your heart to all of those in need of a boost with a positive charge. Melt the selfish and mean streak that all of us have from time to time. Let go and let the love grow, the love we leave behind when we show what's in our hearts that are not selfish and mean. Leave the old way of thinking that was selfish and mean, in which nothing grows.

Have fun and enjoy your life and spread love. It will grow and grow to all those you touch. How do you make them feel? Treat others the way you want to be treated, and you will be treated the same way. Be the way you see it to be. Love with all your heart; help the brokenhearted by the things you do and say. Encourage others, and others will encourage you.

Love is the best medicine you can give anyone.
It's more than a four-letter word; it's a six-
letter word and that is action.
Everyone sees what you do, with no words spoken; you just do.

Love ... is in action, more than words spoken but lived out loud.

CHAPTER 11

Hurt

Watch what kids are doing, but don't ride them about everything they are doing. Why not join in what they are doing and stand beside them instead of criticizing them in what they are doing? They are learning what to do and having fun and enjoying what they are doing. Listen to what they say, and learn what they like and dislike. They are on a journey, just as we are. Children learn by our example. Be a good example for them to learn by.

Don't try to hurt your children, but when it does happen, own up to it; don't deny it. Give love and ask forgiveness when you've made a mistake. It will mend all things back together that once were scattered all about. It may take time, but they will come back around and love you once again, even when they refused to see all the love you give. Take time and make time to listen and learn before it's too late, and they won't want to listen.

It's hard to talk to someone who won't listen to you. You'll see when they were trying to speak to you, and you wouldn't listen. Know things have changed, and it's their turn to listen, but they won't hear the words that are being spoken now.

No one has time to listen to others anymore. The only time they chose to listen is when the hearts are broken and lives are tossed around like a jigsaw puzzle. Your emotions are left in the dust and soon begin to rust; then you want to bust. Take a moment and pick up the phone and really listen to what others are saying. Don't just pretend you care about what they're saying until you get off the phone and then forget all the words that were spoken.

Talk about what they like and what they would like to do, and encourage those—help them see their dreams come true. Life is too short to make it all about you, and who cares about what you need? We all need someone sometimes, more than you know until the person is gone. Now it's too late to listen. Now that you want to listen, you have no voice to hear. All that's left is a tear, but now the priorities are made perfectly clear.

Everyone has a broken heart that cuts down deep; you want to leap. You could hear in their voice, if only you took time to listen and not just blow them off. You didn't take time to listen and accept them the way they are and all the things that are shining bright on their hearts. Hear their dreams and their wishes and hopes for their tomorrows; those are the words spoken today. You know the ones you love to share with, the ones you love, and friends.

People don't want to take the time to listen. It's because it cuts into what's happening in their own worlds, and they don't have time to listen to what's going on in someone else's world. We all have hurts that need to be heard, instead of when things are happening, and you're thrown to the curb to deal with it on your own.

In some cases you can deal with it on your own but in some instances not. You need someone to listen and help you through. When others won't listen to you, it's because there was a time when you wouldn't listen to them. You didn't make the time.

It is a cycle that goes around and around; in the end no one will be around. We need to quit kidding around and start being around for our kids. Listen and quit fussing around with this or that when our kids need us the most.

Instead of putting the kids in front of the TV set or in front of the computer to play games to babysit, we need to interact with them. We need to teach them and to let them be kids to enjoy what life has to offer them, instead of violence and crime with bullets flying all about, with the name-calling covering up all the pain and hurt they are afraid to show; with no love whatsoever. What's this world coming to, forgetting what to do, and that is to love?

Knowing how to treat others is more
important than what you do for them.

Kids grow up to fast. Know what they really want to do. They are thrown out the door before their feet can touch the floor and cast away like they weren't even there.

It hurts to know you were there, and you sat with no emotions or caring about all the pain that was handed out. It's time to stop and take a stand for what it right and stomp out what's not right. It starts with listening in the beginning when someone is talking to you. Stop and really listen. It can make or break someone's spirit by not listening. Talk about what they're doing right, and don't focus on what they're doing wrong. Don't ride them about everything they do. Stand beside them; get involved in what they are doing. Help erase all the hurt that has been caused by no one taking time to listen.

Accept others as they are. No one needs to be perfect to be loved. Be who you are; we're all unique and divinely the way we are. If we need a little change, God will do the change. Life changes a little bit when you have children. You teach, and they learn and love as they grow to be who they are—a child of God whom he has created us to be.

Share in all the blessings he has sent for us to enjoy and not destroy by the actions we take and the responsibility that needs to be taken. Love and nurture and celebrate in all the new things they learn as they grow.

They never saw it before now. They experience it one day at a time and enjoy. See the smiles grow wide and wider as time goes on, as love touches them deep as they let out a peep. Encourage all their dreams to come true and the adventures of a lifetime that are ahead of them. Reach for the stars, even when you fall and get a few battle scars. Get up and go again; life is not always fair. Sometimes it's a little rocky from time to time, but we need to keep on moving forward and climb some valleys that tend to be overwhelming. Go to someone who will listen to you—your mom, your dad, or a friend who has seen the light.

When they listen to you in the beginning, they will listen to you until the end—as well as the middle of life's scary times, the trials with no denial, and the tests that we all go through.

No one needs to hurt the way they do. Don't wait until it's too late to help. Give it first. It only takes a moment to erase all the hurt by one ear and a kind and tender voice that shows you really care.

Take time to make time before it's too late to make a difference.

Love with all your heart, and bring joy to hurt hearts, Think about the little smiles that look up to you. They want to learn and want to be heard in the little world of theirs.

When trying to fit into this big world, listen closely.

You can help with lending an ear and drying a tear, by being near. The love you are giving by listening is healing the hurting. The moments you are taking, giving love, and the actions will speak more than all the words spoken. It will begin to erase all the hurt, and it will show how much you care.

The time taken out of your day to really listen will change a life that is broken. That will last a lifetime; make a difference—the choice is yours. A moment in time can take away a tear down the road by the ear you lend today. In taking time to listen to others today, others will take time to listen to us tomorrow.

Choose to listen; it will change a life as well as yours.

Chapter 12

Heart Feels

When you look back over your life from where you've been to where you are going, it seems different than you could have ever imagined it would be. Actually, it is far better than you ever imagined for yourself.

Each day is a blessing to be where you are,
more than you'll ever know.

Be glad that each day we don't know what the future holds for us. It is like a huge adventure as each moment changes by the choices and decisions we make. Listen to your heart. It will lead you and guide you to the right path for you to take. The only way to know is to make right decisions today, and the peace you feel in your heart when the decisions are made. If it's right for you, you'll have a sense of peace; then you'll know it's right.

The wise choices you make today will bring wise results tomorrow. Think it through, and ask yourself questions, and listen to your heart as you are guided through. Sometimes life throws you curves that you aren't expecting. It comes out of left field, and you're blindsided. Keep believing and moving forward with your head up, and take whatever life throws at you with a grain of salt. Make the most of what you have been given, and take it and make it into something far greater than you could ever have imagined it to be.

Life is a huge adventure when you are kids; you're more in the game, and you understand the concept better than we do as adults. You don't realize that at the time, not until you're in the middle of the game of life. Then life throws something at you that will bring you down to earth, instead of floating up in the clouds. It's a giant wake-up call.

Live in the moment. The people in your life are on a journey as well. No one gets a free ride. We all have tests and trials that we go on. How we treat others and ourselves has a lot to do with the way things turn out in our lives. Our attitudes play a big part in how many times we get to take the test and how long we stay. Be happy, and the longer you will be there. If you change your attitude, the easier it will be on you and others around. Don't think others don't have tests and trials because they do. There are different forms. We just don't see them, but there are. Know in your heart there are.

No one gets to ride free and slip through the raindrops. We're all on the same journey of life together. The raindrops that come splashing down on our hearts filled our buckets at one time. You felt like you were about to go underwater, and you can't come up for air. But in time, you do come up for air. Each step you take, you catch a glimpse of sunshine through the clouds. Your head is still spinning at times when you think of what just happened.

We're here to help others and get our minds off ourselves. The more we think about how we need to help ourselves, the more selfish we become toward others at the same time. By helping others, we actually are helping ourselves. It comes full circle when we help others. God will help take care of us at the same time. We are nothing apart from God. We cannot do anything. Realize that we have nothing to prove to each other, that we are all on a journey together.

We need each other every step of the way. We all have something to give that God has bestowed in all of us; we are to share our love with each other. God loves us, and we should appreciate all that he has given us to share with others. God throws curves and tests at us to keep us close to him. Lean on him and rely on him for everything you need. Share with others what he has already given you to share. Be generous to others, and others will be generous to you. It is a circle of life that goes around and around.

Whatever you sow, you will reap. The decisions you make affect your children and others around you. So make wise ones today. You will know you made the right ones today because of the results that will show up tomorrow.

The truth will take care of it. The lies you say and the things you do are because you think hiding the truth is for the best. But the bigger the lie, the harder it is to make it right. So it's always best to face the truth head-on and get the pain over with right away, instead of letting it linger on and on until it manifests into something that is far out of reach until you begin to deal with it. It will never go away until it has been dealt with head-on, such as fear and what you hide from in fear. It will always be there until you deal with what you fear; then it will be clear. No more living in fear when you face what you feared head-on. It will free you to move on to what has been holding you back. Go for it; you will have much to gain by holding your head up and going through.

Choose to deal with it, now or later; it's up to you. Remember later always comes. When it does, you will be better prepared for the later decisions that you need to make by the wise choices today. Do the work on the upfront then. When the time is right, you'll be able to enjoy the labor of your work down the road. Too much fun up front and less work will give you less time to enjoy later when you're older.

Have balance; it's the only way to get you where you need to be without going overboard in either direction. It gives you peace of mind that you did what you needed to do. We all have choices to make daily, to forgive the ones we love. It's the only way to live in peace and harmony with each other. We all make mistakes, and what we take from them is our choice—to go forward makes us who we are.

Believe in others as you begin to believe in yourself. Things come up; change of plans, go with it. Ride the storm out, and see the outcome from it. Your outlook will be broader than ever before. There was something you needed to learn from this change of plans. You become bolder and much wiser and stronger when you faced your fears. As you learn to be wiser, you'll become kinder and bolder as you get older. Trust God with all your heart and mind.

Your heart feels love with it; you will.

CHAPTER 13

It's about Forgiveness

I t starts within; forgive yourself before you begin
The race and the steps you take to make things all right to move on.

When your heart is broken, when words are spoken,
Let it go and forgive, and the love will spring wide open.

It helps more than you will ever know; until you take that step and forgive yourself Something will be missing.

It will change your life in a heartbeat by just forgiving.

The joy and love will fill you up like something you could only imagine. It's amazing how better you feel when the pressure has been lifted off your shoulders, and you are free to love again. It took me a while to begin again. The lesson's learned but not forgotten; the first thing was to release myself from all that stuff I had stuffed down deep in my soul that needed to come out, once and for all, by letting myself off the hook.

Take a long look at all the things you have been caring around for way too long that have been eating you alive inside, and you have been acting out. Take a long look inside; things will be revealed about you that you didn't know, that you were trying to hide—the guilt and the condemnation that you've felt each time things didn't go well.

I've held grudges against myself for not standing up and doing the right thing the way I thought the way things should be done.

Everything turned out okay. Things don't need to be perfect to be right. We are harder on ourselves than we really need to be. Life is too short to live so narrow-mindedly. There is a big world out there for us to enjoy.

Why not enjoy every moment of the day? It's time to let go of all the anger in our hearts and the grudge match with ourselves and others. It's not worth all that extra unnecessary roughness and the underlying current that has been buried down deep. All the pain we've brought down on ourselves needs to be released. It will change our hearts and the entire notion we think we needed by holding onto that grudge.

Stand up and begin to budge, and forgive and let go of the grudges. It takes courage, but you can do it. You will be glad you did. Take that first step, the leap of faith, and you will get released from all that added pressure that you have been under. All the unforgiveness buried down deep will be wiped clean as soon as you let go and forgive.

I used to beat myself up all the time, trying to keep others on top and happy at my expense, and that made no sense. It used up all my defenses. Things would erupt when things didn't go well. It was hard to please the unpleaseable.

I've learned to take a backseat, let go, and let others be in charge of their own happiness. It's not my place to jump through hoops and run their races. Happiness is made at their own pace, and it's their responsibility not mine or yours. Some times are meant for each of us to experience as we go, and if you don't want to experience it, that's your choice to make. Enjoy being you, and I will enjoy being me. That's the way it needs to be—to be in charge of our own races and the things we need to face as you and me.

Be happy and forgive yourself, and let loose and be free as a goose at last. What a blast from the past, when you had no fear, only fun and great cheer that was going to last.

Happy you'll be when you let all of it go and
let you hair flow freely in the breeze.

Let go of all your defenses that you have been carrying around with you. Know it is time to give up the ghost that keeps you on your toes and everything in rows; that throws you into a whirlwind; that keeps everything spinning until the end, all uptight in knots, feeling there is no way out. There is a way out through to the other side of the mess we get ourselves into in due time. It will be turned and made right without a fight over who is right and who is wrong. It's up to you.

By not letting go, you have a fight, but when you let it go, it will be just right. You wouldn't think letting go would be the ticket the whole time. It was there the whole time but you didn't knowing it. You do have the key to the doors you've been locked. The key to unlocking the door is by walking through the door of forgiveness. If you do, the walls will come down as you forgive. A life will shine bright, and things will be all right.

By forgiving yourself your free as a goose in a noose given a boost from the roost and let loose. Boast about how you can break free from all the abuse you put yourself through. God gives you the strength to forgive and the strength to love from above. Move ahead as you forgive yourself and forgive others. You will be out of the prison where you've been living.

Give yourself a break; don't beat yourself up when things don't go quite right. Remember things happen the way they are supposed to happen, even when it's not the plan we think it needs to be.

It happens even better if we relax and don't worry so much about the outcome of the small stuff. Don't get in a big hurry to get everything done in one day. Save some things for another day, and enjoy yourself.

It gets done, it gets done; if not, that's okay.

Love one another, and have fun with each other. Grow old with each other, laugh, live, and forgive. Most of all, be kind to one another.

Peace, hope, faith, harmony, and love keeps your hearts growing.

Keep this in mind: forgiveness and love go hand in hand. Take a stand. Do one, and you'll do the other. Keep smiling and hoping.

You will see your dreams tomorrow by the things you do today.

Be the best example you can be. Live wholeheartedly. The sky's the limit; it's ready for you to stretch your hand and reach it. You can do anything you put your mind to, if you want to.

Where there is a will, there is a way.

With a can-do attitude, you will see it.

The time is now; don't let someone tell you any different. We all have dreams; we all can reach them if we want to. Forgiveness is something you need to do to be free from things that are holding you back. Letting go of the past at last will allow you to grasp new and wonderful things. It's all about forgiveness. It lets you loose and gives you a boost!

Your future awaits you!

Chapter 14

No Looking Back

Celebrate life with no looking back, no regrets.
God shows us how fragile life is; it can
be gone in a blink of an eye.
God wants us to live life to the fullest with love in our hearts,
as our kids do from the start—always with smiles on their
faces and love and laughter that has been left behind.

Always with a foot to the floor and no looking back, loving
and kind, only looking forward for brighter tomorrows.

Why put off until tomorrow what you can do today?

L ove others while you still can. Don't put it off until tomorrow;
tomorrow maybe too late. Say "I love you" today. Tomorrow
you may wish you could. Start today; tomorrow they may be called
home, and then it will be too late.

Love today. What's in your heart? Let the love you feel be known
before they are called home. Not *wishing* you did but *knowing* you did,
you loved with all your heart, as our kids do from the start.

Express love and know that you loved everyone each and every
day, not wishing you had. Live your life to the fullest without looking
back; love with all your heart.

Go for your dreams as the world goes around. Celebrate life; love
others while you still can, with a hug and a kind word, and do the

best you can. Don't waste a minute on petty things. Forgive them and let things go.

Make every second count. Love them while you still can.

What I've learned most is that life's too fragile to live angry and upset and bent out of shape. If someone is on your mind, and you haven't called or talked to in a long time, don't wait until you read about it; do something about it.

Take time to make time to call.
Send a note or two; give a hug—maybe two or three.
Enjoy all the laughter as you endure the tears throughout the years.
Do what's in your heart; listen to the
whispers of love dancing all around.
Celebrate life and share love with others
before it's too late for them to hear.
Love is to be shared; take time to smell the
roses and make lots of wishes.

Life is too short.

Tell people how much you love and appreciate them today
While you still can.
Celebrate life; no looking back.
Share love.
Look forward to a brighter tomorrow!
No looking back or living with regrets.
Love today as you move forward with happy tomorrows.

No looking back!

CHAPTER 15

Love

In time, love heals all wounds.
You might be left with some battle scars.
That's okay, as long as you have love to see you through.
Everything will work out like brand new.
Battle scars, love mends, through skinned
knees, all you need is love.
All the bars on our hearts like bolted steel
that feel like they will never heal.
But in time they will, with love.
With a drink and in a blink, you will sink into a pit.
But love indeed will pull you out.
Love walks through a fiery storms and
dorms and dreams that come true.
Love has seen all of it.
Love helps you through all the dark and good times; for the
joyful and happy days and all the moments in between.
Love never loses its luster and shine.
Even when you are in the midst of all the pain you go through,
It shines even brighter and stronger than before love.

Love is a mender, a defender.
Not a pretender; love to get what you
want, exactly when you want it.

Real love, you stay long after the goose bumps are gone.
You remain long after everyone has gone home.
You will find that exactly what you needed was love to be shared.

Be kinder and bolder it takes courage more than you know.
You need love to be real and to break the chains of all the fences.

Heal all the bruises and all the cuts down deep with a hug and a kind word of encouragement—the love felt down deep, both by one touch and a soft word spoken. Soon laughter will ring around in the room; light shining all about no doubt.

By love that's been given, now only thoughts remain. It's a revealer of hopes and dreams; keep giving and loving by the way you live. Free to love by the way you give—that's what you need to get started. Start today by the words spoken, it's a token of love. It goes by the wayside, down deep inside. The more you love, decide you're not afraid to show the real feelings. As you love, it begins to grow when you shout out loud. It will glow as it shows by the actions you take.

Love shows it, and you will know it; your heart will feel it when you are the real deal, not some phony, like riding a pony. Be the one who will be remembered long after you passed by. Share the love you have to give. Even when you fall off the horse, get up and get going again.

Love

Put a smile on someone's face once again
By being the real deal!

Chapter 16

No One Can Come Close to the Real You but You

No one can fill your shoes. The one who
is best qualified for the job is you.

It is a lot easier being yourself than you think. You're at peace, the inner peace you can only have and enjoy when you are yourself and not trying to be something you're not.

The more you try, the worse it becomes. Soon you're all upset and everything is in a wreck by not being your true self. No one has seen the real you, not even you. You will begin to surprise yourself by how much better you will feel by being yourself. The peace you will have deep inside will be like nothing you've ever felt before. It is much harder to keep being something you are not than it is being yourself.

Why put yourself through all that agony and defeat by beating yourself up, trying to fill shoes that are not yours to fill and never will be. The only shoes you can fill are your shoes. Let go of those high expectations you have put on yourself to fill shoes that aren't yours but someone else's to fill.

God already knows what he has, because he made you. He loves and cares for you and accepts you for you. Why try to change perfection when you were perfectly made? If God thinks you need adjustments, he's the adjuster, not you or others. Why change into something you are not and you'll never be? Accept who you are, and be all you can be. Don't be afraid to try new things; you can. God will give you the strength and guidance you will need. The most important thing of all is to be the real you, the way God made you, designed perfectly with you in mind.

Love yourself first and everything else falls into line. You really have to love yourself to get anything done in this world.

—Lucille Ball

To fall in love with yourself first is the secret to happiness.

—Robert Morley

Don't break your heart; self-love seems so often unrequited.

—Anthony Powell

Be gentle with yourself, learn to love yourself, to forgive yourself, for only as we have the right attitude toward ourselves can we have the right attitude toward others.

—Wilfred Peterson

Inspire others to love you. The first step on the romance is you. Honoring and loving yourself opens the door for another to truly do the same.

—Rev. Laurie Sue Brockway

CHAPTER 17

Embrace Your Flaws—
We All Have Them

*Accept the ones you have; they make who you
are and the way you will always be.*

God made you special in every way. Accept who you are and stop trying to change the way God intended you to be. No will be able to see the real you until you love yourself just the way you are. Don't give explanations for the things you do or say. We all have special quirks that leave marks on our hearts, and it's okay.

Let go of all that pain that is holding you back, not allowing you to be the real you. It's time to step out of the box you've put yourself in and get to living the adventure of a lifetime by being the real you, the one who isn't afraid to run in the rain, even in the midst of all the pain, and who isn't afraid to show the tears from your heart—that's a start. Let you hair flow through the air as you dance around in the rain. It's freeing as you learn to let go of all the things that have been keeping you sitting still for too long.

No more sitting around and watching the world going around while putting your life on a shelf because you haven't lived up to others' expectations—and yours as well. Let go of all that nonsense that makes no sense, of being someone else. Be all you can be. Let your hair down and your walls of expectations that no one can ever live up to.

It's time to go onward and be all you can be. Who cares what others say about you? Get to living with your heart wide open, and let all the love in, as well as let all the love out—the love deep down inside of you that is ready to come out and shine. Let all the true colors out in full bloom for others to see, like a rainbow floating across the sky after a summer shower.

If you can learn to love yourself and all the flaws, you can love other people so much better. And that makes you so happy.

—Kristin Chenoweth

Love yourself unconditionally, just as you love those closest to you, despite their faults.

—Les Brown

Love yourself instead of abusing yourself.

—Karolina Kurkova

When you allow yourself to compromise you, you will begin to allow others to do the same. It escalates over time—until you are on the downward spiral, and you hit bottom so hard, and it hurts so bad your heart is broken into a million little pieces.

God gives you a giant wake-up call and says, "Are ready to live the life that Jesus died to give you?" It is time to sit up and take notice of what's going on around you. You're beating yourself up for no reason by thinking if you do everything just right, that will make everything all right.

No, it will not. Trying to be something you are not is like a puppet on a string with a ring. You think you have to be the perfect queen or king, in whom everything has to be perfect to be right. If you make everything perfect on the outside, then it will be okay. Wrong, because on the inside your heart is falling apart. It started to shatter the first time I compromised who I was into something I wasn't. I tried to keep everyone happy and tried to be the fixer of everyone's problems, which I had no business doing in the first place. At the time, it distracted me enough to keep me occupied with someone else's mess.

In the meantime, I pretended everything was perfect in my little world, but mine was in a big mess as well. I helped others so I could escape what I needed to do in my life. I didn't want to hurt others by saying no; y saying yes all the time, I was hurting myself in the process. I needed to give myself a recess without being stressed. As I was hurting in the process, I hurt others and didn't even know it until the damage was done. I didn't have the courage to face what was going on inside of me. I avoided it until I couldn't avoid it any longer. The more I put it off, the harder it became to stand up for myself.

At the same time, I lost *me* in the process by doing what others had expected me to do, what I'd always done. I was the fixer of all things, but the only thing I couldn't fix was me, as well as keeping others around me happy as I'd always done, trying to make our son well. I was wearing too many hats to count. I began to blame myself for things I couldn't fix. I thought if I jumped through all sorts of hoops, it would work this time. But each time it never worked—and it never will.

God showed me I'm not the fixer of all things; he is. I needed to believe and trust him with all things, and he would take care of all things that need to be fixed. It was time to let myself off the hook; it wasn't my job to make others happy and keep them happy. It is their choice to be happy or not. It's not my job (or yours) to make sure they are happy, even when they chose not to be.

Over time, I developed the habit that if others around me were happy, I would be too. To keep everyone at happy and upbeat and at peace is a never-ending battle. It isn't your job to fill; it is God's job. He's the pillar of strength. He gives us the strength for what we are supposed to do, not for what others are supposed to do for themselves.

My heart was broken into pieces each day by trying to fill shoes that I couldn't fill. My broken heart needed mending. When our son was diagnosed with a life-threatening illness, I blamed myself for his illness. I thought it was my fault, but it really wasn't. Things began in my mind, and it went from there. Slowly, after time; I began to hate myself even more for things that were out of my control. It is so mind-boggling. The more I tried to change into something that I wasn't, the worse I treated myself and others around me. God showed me that I needed to accept myself for who I was and not be so hard on myself when things didn't go the way I expected them to go.

Let go of the high expectations of trying to fix everything and make everything perfect. It will be better for you and others around you. Everyone has choices to make, and you can't make those choices for them. It's up to them to make choices and live with them. You can't change what others say or do, but you can take responsibility for what you do. By doing so, you will be free to be you, the real you.

I didn't realize I was doing that, and it also showed how I was treating others the same way. Out in public, I pretended everything was perfect and just peachy. In the meantime, my inside was crying as I was denying and dying inside. I didn't like what was going on, but I didn't know how to handle it any other way. I was burying it. I kept saying to myself, *Someday I will run away and start anew,* until I had no more space to stuff my stuff. It was overflowing, running over the sides, and ready to explode—and one day, it did.

When God put the mirror in front of me to show the real me, something wasn't quite right. Over time, I hurt myself and others. He loves us and shows us things that are going on around us. You need to love yourself as God loves you because he made you. He knows all about you.

Until you begin to love and accept yourself, even with the flaws, your life will never change. Accept God's love that he has for you, and love your life. Everything begins with love, and that starts with you.

God forgave me; I needed to forgive myself as well—that is the first step—and to be able to forgive others. Everything in life revolves how you treat yourself and others; it makes the world go around.

Love and give love, each and every day.

To love yourself right now, just as you are, is to give yourself heaven. Don't wait until you die. If you wait, you die now. If you love, you live now.

—Alan Cohen

I don't like myself; I'm crazy about myself.

—Mae West

Each day I'm learning to love myself as God does. Life is a lot brighter each and every day, now that love is near and God is here, closer, and helping me let go of all my fears. I know he loves and really cares for me. Let go of the past; learn from it. Move on from it; don't camp out there. You will stay there; it's best not to go there. You've been there long enough.

You can't change what has already been. Look what's up ahead, not what lies behind. It is what it is.

Keep moving one step at a time, and enjoy every step you take on the way to where you are going next. Each day is a beautiful for you to enjoy, even the rainy days. Remember the sun always comes out tomorrow to enjoy today.

Celebrate who you are, and enjoy everyone around you.

To love and be loved is awesome; be a part of and share with others as well as yourself. Have fun while you are dancing in the rain, even in the midst of the storm. Remember: this too shall pass; it doesn't last. Each day is a brand-new day for all of us to enjoy. Write a new page for our story today to remember tomorrow. So make a memorable and a positive day that brings laughter and tears to all who hear.

Go out and do your best, and let God take care of the rest. Know that you are the best you can be. Have fun on your journey. The greatest adventure to be on is being yourself for others to see—the real you. No more pretending about it; no matter what, this is me.

CHAPTER 18

No One Can Come Closer than Me

Don't change the light that is burning inside
For someone else's fire that went out long ago.
Try to put your fire out, so you can be just like them.
Changing you, but not loving you.
A light shining bright, for who are you?

The number-one thing to remember is to be you. No need to impress; more you do, the worse it gets, and the worse you feel as the impression takes place. It doesn't work to try; each one of us is one and the same. No need to impress others. It gets you nothing but heartache and pain. You'll put yourself into an awkward situation for no reason at all. In the long run, you'll hurt yourself alone. It's not worth all that nonsense.

It is best to be yourself. The more you are, the better you will feel and heal. Be the real you, not the one you pretend to be, in which you have to impress, and you need to be in competition with others. You think you have to have what others have before you can be happy. The more you try, the more you deny as you go after what others have and the worse everything turns out to be, not what you think it's supposed to be.

The real you—when you let go of all that nonsense, the freer you'll become, and you will be what God intended you to be—you.

The more yourself you are, the more real your life becomes. You'll see the real colors around you. Be the real you, and life begins to make more sense.

Others will be more intrigued by who you really are, by being yourself, than they ever were when you were trying to impress them. That gets you nowhere and only hurts you when you live in despair, and you want to disappear.

Dare to be the real you; that's where your real life begins and the fun never ends, an adventure of a lifetime. Everything changes; nothing stays the same. You learn day by day, moment by moment. Take a look around, and you'll see and learn so much and experience more by being yourself than you ever did by being something you are not.

The future has something for you to learn; it's yet to come. Dare to be yourself; you have a lot to see and fun adventures to come. Step out to be the real you. You'll have fun by being the real you and enjoying what's yet to come. You won't regret a thing; in fact, you'll enjoy everything your life has to offer by being yourself.

Remember that life reflects how you treat the real you, not the pretend you. Yu have so much to give be being you. Let the real you shine. No one comes closer to the real you than you. Keep shining and smiling, and be the real you.

Make your mind up; it will happen. Be the real you! Have fun by being you.

CHAPTER 19

Angels from Above

Angels sent from heaven, angels sent from above.
Angels sent for you and me.
Angels sent to spread joy along the way.
To sprinkle love on everyone they meet along the way.
Angels also touch our hearts in a special way.
Their love passes right through to another broken heart.

The angels speak softly to our souls that last
a lifetime to the brokenhearted.
Little angels show you more in the little time
they are here than searching in a lifetime.
When you think you're alone and you feel afraid,
then look to the sky for comfort and joy.
When you feel the joy rise up in your heart,
and as the healing pours down like rain,
Sweet memories remain, and through time cannot be erased.
Your heart feels aching, and a river begins to
fall, as your back is up against the wall.

Remember the good times that we all shared.
In time, when the angels are called, heaven awaits
to welcome them home once again.
It's hard to see them go, when it's time for them to go.

Little angels will watch from afar up above and see you through.
The light shines down on you and me.
Touches our souls down deep, as we weep, as we drift off to sleep.

We heal from the inside out, through time and days on in,
Soon you will visualize the world in a different
way, through your angels' eyes.
Angels sent from heaven above.

CHAPTER 20

Hope

What are you hoping for in life?

Are you hoping for a better way to live, a better job, a better car, and a house? You see, the possibilities are endless with materialistic items. How you view your life and what you hope for go hand in hand. Remember you have only one life, and that's yours to live.

God gives us hopes and dreams and desires in our hearts on the day we are born. It's up to us to live out loud, to be all we can be, and not what others think or say we ought to be.

To live to our full potential, we have inside us the real you and me that wants to come out and shine for others to see. We need to hope for more than what we see about you and me.

What does your life look like right now? What do you see? Do you see all your heartache and pain? Do you see darkness and restlessness? Do you sleep less in your space? Others have hurt you and called you all sorts of names, and you want to run away and hide. But wherever you go, the words keep going off in your head, rolling over and over in your mind, and you can't escape from all those words. One by one, they get louder and louder; there is no denying when you are lying.

Each day it gets a little bit darker, and your heart begins to get harder and harder. You're about to reach the point of no return. You decide in the pit of darkness to pitch a fit, and you are the one to get hurt—and the innocent ones also. Your head starts to make plans to take matters in your own hands from all the hurts from day one.

It will come out all at once—all the things you have buried. You've reached the boiling point, and others refused to see the signs—withdrawn from class, the change of behavior, change of hair color, a changed demeanor. Today is the day you've decided you can't tolerate one more day, and you want to take action. You don't know what to do. You've tried to talk and reach out to others, but no one has the time.

A short time later, a small voice says, "Don't stoop to their level to get back at them. That's my job. I'm your vindicator, and I'll take care of it."

The choice is yours. You're going at it the wrong way, and you know it in your heart in that split second when you choose to stop.

Everyone needs to be heard. Teachers don't listen, and parents are too busy to care—until it is too late, and you're all ready at heaven's gate. Then you'll sit up and listen, but then it's too late.

Now you have the time; if only you could get back the time you lost. The "if only" keeps playing over and over in your head.

Others are too busy to take time to really hear what others have to say. If they do listen, it's only to say, "You're reading it all wrong," or "It's your imagination running away with you," and "They wouldn't do that to you."

There's no concept that something is truly is going wrong. They say you are being overly sensitive about school, and you're just being a baby about the whole name-calling thing. We all go through that.

When it happens to you, being bullied is no fun. When it happens to you, it's a whole different story.

Words cut down deep, and it hurts more than you know. We should sit up and take notice of what is going on in our schools, neighborhoods, and homes. Others don't know or seem to care to want too. Its your life take control its time to take a stand.

Walk away from those fools who make up all those rules. You are special in every way. God intended you to be unique, just the way you are. Who says that you need to change? If you need to change, God will do it. Who cares what others think? Leave all the scars behind, and rewind, and go forward.

Take a stand, or blow up your future and others' as well by sitting back and doing nothing, and watch everything unfold right in front of you. When you sit around and do nothing, you are just as guilty as the ones who did it—you could have done something.

You chose to turn your back on someone who needed your help. You turned your head and walked away; you didn't want to get involved because it might upset the apple cart and hurt your reputation with the in-crowd.

What a joke. The in-crowd likes to hurt others to make themselves look big. You don't want to involve yourself because you might get hurt yourself. You don't realize that by not helping others, you are actually hurting yourself more than if you would have helped others in the first place. It's like a lion that came to conquer and devour everyone in his path, including you and me.

No one wins until someone takes a stand; if not, you will fall for everything. If the school and parents won't listen, why would the kids? It's all about, "Should we do this, or should we do that?" The kids don't know which way to turn. It's like a going on a merry-go-round and trying to get off.

Once you do, your head is still spinning around, trying to get your marbles all straight. Your heart is going one direction, and your head is going another to face all the stuff that comes your way. No wonder everything is a mess. Everyone is trying to be like everyone else, or you are no one. That's odd and a little offbeat and out of sync, don't you think? Or don't you even see that everything is off key with you and me?

Why would you like to be like someone else, always hurting others? It's like a vicious circle of being cruel and trying to rule and hurting the world all around us, your family and friends. Who can bash who first, who can we hurt today and get another notch on our belts and put another lipstick print on another forbidden lip?

Nothing will change until we sit up and take notice of what's really going on. Take a stand and start loving once again, and let go of all the bashing and hashing all around. The Bible says to love others as you love yourself. But if you don't love yourself and accept your unique and divinely designed self, with you in mind, you are missing out on the best quality you have in life, and that's you.

So let's start today, and let go of the world's idea of designing us to be like one another. Learn to be more like our Creator intended us to be—more like him. Love and enjoy one another's gifts and talents and our special quirks we have been given to share. Don't be like one another, but love and accept one another as we are.

Don't be the way you think you need to be in order to be liked, where everyone is in charge of everything because you think you are better than everything. That's so wrong to think that way.

To get back at everyone for what has been done to you is a fatal position to be in.

It's best to leave it to God. He is the redeemer, and he is the battle claimer. Leave the job to him when others come against you. It will be hard to walk away, but it will turn out just right. When you take matters in your own hands, it turns out upside down and all in a big mess with a wreck and a headache and pain.

Put your hope in the Father above. He will change everything for the better. No matter what it looks like right now, in due time, keep your faith and believe he has it all covered. He knows what's best for you and that you can trust him with all the promises. He will change it all around for you and me.

Keep your faith and believe, no matter what it looks like right now. So when words are spoken out of hate and cuts down deep, choose not to listen and just walk away. Remember those words are coming at you to hurt you, but God is here to protect you and deliver you onto a brighter path. Your future awaits you. Keep your head up, keep walking forward, and be stable. He gives you the power to stay strong, even when the heat really comes on to tear you down. God's kingdom is to be the real you; the world is to be like everyone else. Put your hope in God. He has your best interests in mind. He has designed you and will not deny you. He knew you before anyone else. You are a masterpiece, made with his hand. So why try to alter his creation. All his creations are awesome and that includes you and me. God's plan for you up ahead is so amazing.

Remember these are lessons, some hard and some not so hard. It's not so hard to stand up when you see others being beaten down to the ground and when you put yourself in their shoes. It could have been you. It's God's good grace and mercy; you are not. Stand up for the weak and injustice for others. That's part of our tests as well.

Be like others, or to stand up for others—the choice is yours. What you sow today you reap tomorrow. So don't be a creep and sleep and fall down on your feet and begin to weep. Help someone who's been in defeat.

Be the hope they need by being you and me.

So don't have a stroke by being one of those folks who steps aside as you hide.

But step out, and don't be afraid.

Be the real you that's buried down deep inside.

Stability shows ability.

Walk in love for others to see the real you; don't just say it but live it; it means more than just saying it.

Indeed sow a seed, and you will reap.

Be the change you want the world to be.

The seed indeed to fill the need, and that's the way it needs to be.

Spread love and hop and joy around through you and me.

Today make a difference in someone else's life!

Live out loud with love in your heart.

Watch and see if somebody is in need.

Help get it done; what a wonderful seed indeed by filling a need.

When people lose hope, their lives are over, and everything stops. It's like the fire has gone out. The sparks have slowly faded away into the darkness of their pain, and the tears just won't come when they have lost hope. We're all here to fan the fire in others who have lost hope in their lives. Take a stand and encourage others, and love them through time. We have sat on the sidelines long enough, doing nothing and watching others getting discouraged and running and telling everyone what has been going on. Don't you realize we all lose when we think and treat others in that manner? We would be lost and forgotten by being so rotten. This is real life, true stuff, and life is tough. And when you stuff your stuff, we all need love and acceptance. When a life is taken, it's forever, and there are no do-overs. Wishing you can start again is a waste of time, wishing your life away.

That moment in time you made a wisecrack or a hateful gesture. It could be the one that sets the ball rolling downhill, falling from there. All the stuff they hear from day one may be too much for them to take. It's a downhill spiral that can affect more than one.

Remember you cannot help what others do, but you have a choice in what you do. The actions you take can make a difference in someone else's life, as well as your own. Listen to your heart, and say something nice. It will mean a lot in so many ways. not only for you but for the one you are speaking to. It can mean a life saved or a life taken by the words spoken. Know in your heart you can make a difference by the good and loving choices you make.

In the past, it was drugs, sex, and rock and roll. We are good to roll and don't fold. Look forward to peace and harmony on the go. Love and help each other to grow. Now, where did all that love go that we once knew?

Now it's drugs, text let's all have sex, get ahead and no one gets fed or led, no peace only chaos, jet-speed ahead, rock and roll, fall out of school; it is cool. Have babies and leave them standing on the landing. It's one for one, all for one, and there's no love at home or on the road to nowhere, and no one cares for anyone anymore, only for themselves.

"If you keep biting and devouring each other watch out or you will be destroyed by each other" (Galatians 5:15).

"You, my brothers, were called to be free but do not use your freedom to indulge the sinful nature, rather, serve one another in love" (Galatians 5:13).

"The entire law is summed up in a single command: 'Love your neighbor as yourself'" (Galatians 5:14).

Ask God to come into your heart and fill you up with his love and truth. Your life that once was filled with darkness will be filled with his light. Your life will be forever changed, and it will never be the same, but it will be all right.

Ask for forgiveness. He will give you all the grace and favor and love and truth you will ever need—enough that you can share with others. Share your story of how he changed your story from darkness to light with your fright. Make a new start with a brand-new heart; you are smart. You have a heart and lots of love to give. You don't need to take your life to escape. Let yourself off the hook. Relax and be yourself; that's all it takes, no more fakes. Do your best, and leave the results up to him.

Be you the way God intended you to be—the real you. You don't need to alter your looks, to fill the books, to have new looks to fit in. You will never be something you were never meant to be. You are special, and you've had a beautiful heart from the start.

Use the tools that God gave you and me. First, walk away if you need to, if you don't like what you hear. Don't act like someone else; be you. Use the wisdom he has bestowed in you.

Dream!

Your life and your hopes and what you care about will show in you.

Love!

It/s best when it is given and not hidden; you're not living when you're not giving love.

Show it and give it, and have fun with it. You're really living.
Don't live in regret by not showing love; we all need it.
It works better by giving it and not just saying it, but giving and living and loving.
Live with hope and share it; tomorrow will be brighter and lighter than today.

Love and don't hide in the shadows of darkness, but live in the light burning bright in your heart tonight.

Dare to be different, free to be you.
That's all I have to say—go for it; you will be glad you did!
Love out loud; it will be the change you need.
The real you!
In hope you'll find by being kind.

Change a life by listening today.
It will change you as well in the long run by the choices you make today.
In time it will pay off in years to come, down the road.

Once you do, it is the best news, by all the clues. It's best to let go of all the rules, and act like fools sitting on the stools. The one who makes the rules has no clue what to do and sits, choosing to do nothing to help out. Stand out and don't blend in. We have plenty of them. Sit up and take notice; you are amazing and wonderfully made, a beautiful heart to share the light. Others who are in the dark need others to show them the light that is burning in your heart tonight.

Love and truth will set you free to be you the real you.

CHAPTER 21

Yourself

S tep out of the box—the "afraid box" that you have put yourself in to hide. It's time to let it all go and try something new. Begin again; it's fun being the real and wonderfully made you. Your unique self is full of colors and laughter, as God intended you to be. Act like yourself, and you won't miss a thing as the time rings on.

See the light shining bright in your heart tonight without fright. Have fun—be free to be the real you. Don't be someone else that's pretending to be you.

You're afraid of all the scars in your heart, so you decide to hide them so no one can see them. You put on a mask so you won't have to reveal the pain you feel down inside. You've done it for so long you've grown numb to your life and to others around you.

The walls have gone up after time, and you've become so afraid you don't know what to do or how to let go of all the darkness you have painted on your heart from the start. God whispers in your heart, "Step forward out of the box you've put yourself in. You have so much to give. Why keep it locked up in that box?"

You can choose to shine or to be left behind as you wine and dine on self-pity. This isn't the real you; it's a phony imitation of who you really are. You're special.

It's time to stand as you land, and move forward into tomorrow. Paint a new life, a new story for yourself, full of bright and wonderful colors to enjoy. With redemption, grace, and renewal of your mind, every day has wonderful news.

Jesus loves us every one of us. He died for all of us so we can live. Jesus sacrificed a lot out of love, and so should we share the blessed gift of love with others, as he did. Live in love and harmony with one another. It's the best gift of all. Do your best; that is all he asks of us. It's good news to share.

Stop beating yourself up, climbing the walls of yesterday, and reliving the past mistakes you made, which ended last night. We all make them; you're not the only one who makes mistakes. The slate has been wiped clean. Jesus wiped it all clean for all of us on Calvary.

Christ has risen! Yes, indeed.

He has changed the world and brought light to the darkness and has made it a better place. Take notice, and see what he has done in your life. The blessings, one by one, are amazing.

Whatever you need to focus on and whatever you need to do is up to you.

Have fun being yourself—what an awesome adventure of a lifetime, full of bright colors to share!

CHAPTER 22

Your Future Shining Bright

G et to livin' and be forgiven and lovin', instead of sittin' and
mopin' about things that have been happenin'. That's got your
life spinning out of control. Around and around, things begin to rot
on the spot with all your thoughts in spots that once you thought you
forgot and now is brought to the surface. What needs to be forgiven
are the words spoken yesterday.

It's time to get in gear and stop sitting on your rear, full of fear,
which gets you nowhere quick. It only makes you sick as you take a
look at the book of your life of not forgiving and unhappy thoughts.

Give yourself a lift and forgive and forget and move on and get
going. Going forward has its rewards; don't go in reverse, where
everything is rehearsed over and over in your mind, and everything
gets worse. Your future is right and bright ahead of you. What you
make of it is up to you.

Your attitude is everything. Instead of crying the blues and
having no clue what to do, get up on the inside. All things will begin
to slip-slide, and the rules will change by doing something rather
than doing nothing. Do something you've always wanted to do. You
will see it come true for you, one day at a time.

Your future is shining and bright. Take a look at your life and
see it looks bright. You have nothing to be afraid of. All you need is
to believe. Look what's up ahead, as God says. Don't look at what's
behind you—that will keep you stuck in a rut—as Lot's wife in the

Bible did when she looked back and turned to a salt block and stayed there, solid as a rock, after God said not to look back.

As John Wayne said, looking back is a bad habit to get into.

Keep looking forward and reaching your full potential, which God has placed in the heart and soul of each one of us. We all have things in our hearts that we desire. Listen closely to it. You will achieve them, one step at a time, even when you fall and things begin to close in.

Don't be afraid to get up and get going again.
Your future ahead is shining bright.

Keep moving forward. Don't look at what's in your rearview mirror where you've already been. Why go somewhere you have already been? You know the results and the outcome. Why not see what's up ahead, even when the pressure is on and things get hard.

Don't fold and give in and go backward to where you came from. You have what it takes to get where you need to go, to see your dreams come to pass.

You never fail when you keep going forward. You only fail when you give up and stop trying. Each day, you get up and keep going forward. You're halfway there for your dream to come true for you.

Your future is bright, just as the sunlight.
As your vision, it will be.

Have a big vision and believe it, and you will receive it as you see it.

Your future is shining bright!

CHAPTER 23

Best Medicine

Not telling the truth is like eating fruit that has been on the vine too long. It looks good and sounds good at the time, until you bite into it. It is poison that touches your lips, and you only want to spit it out. The way it felt as it came out of your heart rolled under your skin as you gave in, as dead fruit shriveling on the vine so small. A lie begins to drop off, one right after another. Saying one right after another, you feel you need to keep covering with another lie. You can't stop until all the lies are spoken to cover up another, and all the hearts are broken, and everything is revealed by all the lies spoken. You think you're on top, but you are not, and your stomach is tied in knots.

You can tell one lie that can change your life in an instant. A lie that is spoken is not good medicine. It will lead you to a lot of pain. The poison on the vine by the lies spoken is a token; say no and don't go down that road.

Face your responsibilities. Start with the pain of the truth. It is only an instant but gone after that when you come clean of the lies once spoken. It doesn't linger on any longer by pointing fingers. Take the rap that you didn't want the responsibility for in the first place, so you hid behind the lie. You will find it's best to get it over with and take the best medicine of all. Face the truth as you tell the truth. You will see life in a different light. As your kids see you tell the truth when you make a mistake; they will tell the truth.

Kids see and learn from what we do and say. Always tell the truth, even when it hurts; that's the best kind of fruit to hand out. That is no joke. The best kind of fruit is right off the vine, right in line, and comes out of your mouth, and that is what they hear. The best way out is telling the truth; it's the best route to take. You might be in trouble for a moment by your actions, but not telling the truth can leave scars for a lifetime. To tell the truth is the best kind of medicine that comes from the best kind of root, which has been buried down deep as you sleep.

Tell the truth even when it gets rough and stand tough in the midst of stuff, even when things go through the roof. It's the best kind of proof you have. When you always tell the truth there will be no doubt about it. Your heart will be filled with happy thoughts and no regrets or afterthoughts, and your gut won't be tied up in knots. You told what was right, and the truth is the best medicine in the beginning; it leaves no room for sinning, only grinning, by no sinning and no hiding and denying by lying.

Telling the truth; you will be winning from the beginning, and you can keep on grinning, instead of all the ways you keep your head spinning from one lie to another, which will get you nowhere in a hurry.

Love one another, forgive one another, and always tell the truth to one another. Have fun; there's no reason to lie, nothing to prove by being you. Get into the groove by being you, and tell the truth. You have nothing to lose.

Start today, and tell the truth. It's the best kind fruit you can eat or beat on the street to defeat—the best medicine.

CHAPTER 24

Respect Yourself

Think about yourself before acting out.
There is no doubt you are special.

Do not put out on the first date, thinking this is how you will get a second date or that's what you need to do to receive love. That's a wrong way of thinking.

You are special in every way! Don't give your love away in that manner.

Once you cross that line, the respect in the morning is gone. When you lose respect for yourself, everything else begins to erase. You lose yourself in the shuffle that you once controlled. Then anger sets in because you know that you crossed that line you said you would never cross. A sense of sadness comes over you when you realize you let yourself down. When you cross that line one more time, you're going the wrong way, trying to get love in entirely the wrong place with all sorts of faces and cases.

The life you once had is no more; you know there is something deep inside missing. The void you are trying to fill as you stand still you are unable to fill. Somehow, on your own, you're not filling it.

There's yearning and a sense of calm in your soul, with no more eggshells to walk on or having to be something you are not.

Let it go; walk away. It is not worth all that heartache and pain by keeping yourself in a rut. That's not what life is all about, letting others dictate what you should and shouldn't do. Or what you can or cannot do. Who cares what others think or say? It's up to you.

It's time to get to living more boldly and courageous, full of more potential than ever before.

What do you want to do? That's the question. What does your heart say? Take the first step, and do it; you will get through it. You will feel bolder and have more confidence each day. Each step you take makes you stronger than the day before, each time you say no. The first step is hard—the pain of letting go, when you know it's the wisest decision you need to make. By not being a fake, you have what it takes not to be one. Once you take that first step, your eyes will begin to see once again. You know in your heart the path you have chosen to take is in the right direction.

When you stand up for yourself and walk away from something you know is wrong, you realize this isn't for you and let go. Learn from the mistakes, and close the door of all that hatred and the anger that once existed. And let the love remain in you as you do. Learn to forgive yourself for all the unwise choices and decisions made before, and begin to live once again.

Your heart will soften as you forgive often, and you'll gain your self-respect and your dignity, with no turning back from all the new choices and wise decisions you make from this day forward. The more you love yourself and don't punish yourself, the better you will feel. Others will see the results of the how bold and confident you are. It's the *real* you that we love and adore in the way God made you, special in every way. Do not allow someone to tell you any different. You're a child of the Most High, the Creator, the Alpha and Omega. God himself designed you to shine in every way possible. Do not allow someone to change who you are. You're special just the way you are.

When people try to change who you are and won't accept you for who you are, they also won't accept themselves the way they are, one way or another to be like another. Time to walk away. Don't to allow yourself to compromise—that's a bold and wise decision to make. The harder the decision is to make, the more valuable it is to learn. By compromising in the end, you will have to keep it up. People who won't accept you the way you are no friends at all. They have no intention of being your friend; all they want to see is how much you'll do for them—be there for them, go here and there and everywhere for them, be their puppet on a string with no ring but the string. One-sided and always divided, with no love in return.

Walk away; it's the best thing you can do for yourself, without a word spoken. It does no good to speak to someone who refuses to listen and is full of hate and mistreating notions about you. Remember—some will like you, and some will not.

The best thing to do is to keep on walking with your head up and not look back. God will close the doors and open new ones—just for you.

When putting out for the wrong kind of love, you're afraid of being alone and rejected. Don't sell yourself out by giving out. Stop thinking that way. It's not right if you put out to get love in return. "If I do this, they will love me back." When someone truly loves you, he will not ask you to give up the biggest part of yourself to get him to love you.

The person wants to get something from you but is willing to give up nothing for you. That's manipulation and trying to control you by putting a guilt trip on you. That's not love at all. You think, *It's my fault that no one loves me because I didn't give it to him.*

To get to you, they will tell you the words you are longing to hear, knowing full well that after you give in and cross that line, you'll be under their thumb, for being so dumb. In other words, a one-night stand as you land, you will never hear from them. You fell for it once again; you feel so numb for being so dumb to listen to those guilty words. It's time to say no when those negative words put you on that guilt trip one more time.

Don't give in; you'll lose so much more than you'll ever know—
yourself! Being controlled by others is the only way to get what they
want from you, not to love you in any way. That's no life at all. You
lose your self-worth and control to be who you are—the special gem
God has blessed you to be. Once you step out into someone else's
arena, it's not your own.

You will have to keep it up, and you will not get too far in
the stars. You are on a downhill spiral, out of control, to a path of
destruction. It gets you nothing but pain and grief for yourself and no
one else. When you lose yourself, it's hard to get back, but it is worth
every step you take to go forward to get it. Let go of what you can't
change and what others do. You can change what you need to do.
Recover what you have lost, and you will have learned and gained
so much more. It's worth all the cost to get it back.

Stop and listen to your little voice; when it says to stop, it means
stop. Don't think for one minute it will work this time because it
won't. The only thing that will happen is you will get to go around
the mountain one more time. There's no love in return, only in the
moment to get what they want from you but nothing after that. You
will hurt yourself one more time, and you'll be another notch on
their ego chain of life. Put a stop to that way of thinking; it doesn't
work. It only hurts you and no one else.

Remember God loves you just the way you are. No need to
explain all the time. He sees your heart from the start.

Who cares what others think? I know God loves me, even if
you don't. I don't get my self-worth from people. I get it from our
heavenly Father. He will never let me down or leave me on the
ground in front of the crowd, the way others have done.

Put your expectations in the Lord and not in people.

When your expectations are in him, things will begin to turn
around.

God will send you people who love you just the way you are, with no strings attached.

Don't try to get love or use tricks to get love. It will be there. No more trying to get someone to love you. It will be there. It's time to let it go, no matter what you are doing. Nothing will ever change unless you sit up and take notice—before it's too late and your life has passed you by.

Remember some people will love you, and some will not.
It is nothing you did or didn't do.
It is something in them and not about you.

It's not up to you or to me to get them to love you; it's up to them. No need to get back at them; love them anyway, even if they don't love you. You still did what was right, even though it didn't seem right. You shared love in the midst of your pain, even in the rain.

Let it go and move on; be yourself. You have no need to pretend or act like someone else to fit in. Start again, and pick up the pieces, and keep pressing in and pressing on. Life is too short to keep beating yourself up for something that you can't change or rearrange. Don't get love in all the wrong place with so many different faces and in so many case that leave traces. Be yourself. It's not your loss; it is theirs. They are missing out on so much.

God loves me just the way I am, and that's all that matters to me. God will send you others who love you just the way you are. Love others as they are, and soon love will be returned.

No matter what you do, love what you do.
You're free to be who you are—the real you.
Open your heart from the start, and let God in and see the real deal.

He will show you the truth and so many things that you can touch. By letting love in, you will feel real joy and peace. You can enjoy each and every day by listening and obeying that still voice you hear. Stand still and listen closely; it will guide you every moment of the day. Take action when the time comes. Keep on believing and trusting and loving without rushing and crashing as you are dashing through life. But slow down and have fun by being the real you! There's no need to act like someone else to get love; be yourself and show love. Be the love you want to receive by giving it first.

Begin today to respect yourself by being yourself. In a new way, it's a good day to start. The more you respect yourself, the more your life will improve. When you respect yourself and give respect, others will respect you as well. You live what you give.

You give respect; you receive it. Whatever you give, you will reap. Everything begins with you and the moves you make.

If you don't respect yourself, no one else will either. Once you do, everyone else will sit up and take notice by the things you give out. Until you sit up and take notice that enough is enough, you'll know in your heart that something isn't quite right.

Ask God to help you to change, to be helpful and useful to make a difference. The first step is asking for the help you need. Then listen and then act on what he says. Action is the only way anything is going to change. Once you say no and walk away, things will change in a brighter and lighter way. Time to stand up and say *no more*; the storm will cease, and joy will increase, and the sun will begin to shine once again. It takes a little time more. You stand up and don't let others run over you or take control of your life.

It takes courage and boldness. God gives you the strength to be all you can be and do all you can. Even when trials and tribulations come—and they will—this too shall pass. It will be okay; there is something that I need to learn from this that you are going through. He will take care of what you can't, but you have to do your part as well. We both have an equal part in your life. It's not just one-sided, where you have a free ride and no work on your part is needed. Know we are in this together. He will be there to see you through and all the steps of your journey from the beginning until he calls you home.

When things get a little rough and tough from time to time, don't give in and lose ground. When it gets hard and pressure comes on strong, stand up and don't go backward or cross back into old patterns. You've come too far because you already know the outcome—heartache and pain.

Press through when it gets rough. You will be glad you did not give in when it gets a little rocky. Once you give in, the cycle starts all over again, and you'll go around the mountain one more time. You'll lose yourself one more time each time you give in and go around. It gets harder to start again. You are asked to do it and told things will change if you do this or that. Once you do it, it will never happen because you gave all you had and that was yourself. He gave you nothing in return but another broken heart.

When someone really cares about you and loves you for who you are and not what he can get from you, it is genuine from the heart. He wouldn't ask you to give up the biggest part of you, your respect. He respects you enough to give you the freedom to be who you are, the real you.

He knows how special you are and sees you for who you are—not someone you pretend to be but the real you, full of life, and fun to be around and who shows the light. There are no strings to hold you close to the ground. He gives you the freedom to soar like an eagle above the clouds. That's someone you can build a life with. God has someone out there for everyone. Don't compromise to fill an empty promise for the wrong kind of love. That's not love at all. That's being manipulated. "I want it all, and I will give you nothing at all. And watch you fall. Do this, then I will do that. Then I will love you." *Wrong!* the red flag goes up! Don't go there and fall for it. Walk away, and don't compromise yourself.

Remember real love is unconditional. Love with no strings attached is real love. When there are strings of any kind, that's not love at all. Say no and walk away, with your head held up as you walk away. When you have been dating for a long time, you think, *We should be talking about getting married.* You bring up marriage: "What do you think?"

The first thing out of his mouth may be, "We should just move in together." What he is really trying to tell you is he doesn't want to get married; he just wants to sleep with you. By not marrying you, he doesn't have to give up his freedom to be with you.

Freedom is what he is afraid to give up by sharing his love with you. The commitment is something hard for him to make when it is going to cost him the freedom he values the most. He doesn't value you when he asks you to give up the value you have for yourself, the real you. Something he will never get to know is the special person God has intended you to be.

When you think about it, and your little voice is screaming, *Don't do it*, it's trying to tell you something. Part of you knows it isn't right, but the other side says, *Yes, you can make him change his mind in time.* But the reality is you go ahead and move in and give in. He has no reason to change his mind once you give in and hand it over to him on a silver platter.

No work is involved for him; the work was done for him when you gave it to him. He will never have to marry you because you already gave him yourself, and he didn't have to give up anything in return. You gave him everything you had and lost more than you gained. You lost your self-respect and your self-worth by giving in to something you thought was right at the time. Later, you found out it wasn't right at all, and it was all wrong. We have all done this, me included. Sometimes the hardest lessons learned are through an experience. That wasn't love; it was lust that you cannot trust. It will only leave you in the dust. When someone wants you to compromise the shine in you, some way, somehow walk away. You will find it is the best advice you will hear in your life.

Don't compromise for anyone; it is wise not to go there. The feeling is not real; it is only pretend to get you reeled in, and the game begins. They have you right where they want you–in a box all locked up on the dock.

Your self-respect is one of your greatest treasures; it's a gift. Don't make a trade with your greatest gift. You'll get nothing but heartache and pain to claim. The one to blame is you alone; sit up and take responsibility for your actions. That's when you do the healing, it begins and never ends. Your chapter of your journey starts anew.

Face the truth, and get to the root as you go through the fire that's burning down deep inside and has been buried for way too long. That needs to come out and shine.

The decisions and choices you make sometimes you can't take back. But you can live and learn and grow from them. It's all up to you. You can become bitter, or you can come out better and stronger than you were before.

God gives us the freedom of choice to stay right where we are with no change. The more you complain, the more you remain; that's no life at all. The other choice is to step up and step out, and seek the change you want to see; it's up to you. Have a pity party and no fun, or be part of the party and have fun. The choice has been given to you to take it back or sit back and lie idle, do nothing, and keep going around in circles. It stays the same, and the blame game continues. It's up to you to take your self-respect back, even though you have fallen. The first step is the hardest to make; go for it. The best days are yet to come. Each step you make is all uphill, but it becomes easier with each step you take. If it gets hard—and sometimes it does in life—don't fall backward; fall forward. Once you do, everyone else will sit up and take notice. Until you do, no one else will see. Even if they don't, you are not doing it for them; you are doing it for yourself. Take action; it is the only way through the darkness, and the light will begin to appear. Time to stand, time to act; it is the only way to see the change. Let go and move on.

God loves me the way I am; that's all that matters. I don't have to perform to get you to love me. God will send others to love me, just the way I am, no matter what.

Open your heart, and let God in. He will show you so many things and how to enjoy each and every day by listening to your heart. When he says to do or not do something, he is here to help you, not hurt you. He's here to lead you, to guide and nurture you every step of the way to his loving arms.

Your life is more relaxed and lot more fun by being yourself—the real you. No more trying to be something that you are not.

Its time to let go of trying to be a performer at not being yourself. Be who you are, the one God intended you to be, the unique and divine special you—the real you.

Keep trusting and believing and loving, and most of all be the real you. Have fun; you will be able to love yourself more and others in the same way. No more pretending; more living and loving by being yourself. Accept yourself and others just as they are. When you do, the more freeing you become.

You are one of a kind, just as everyone is one of a kind, specially designed with you in mind. No more hiding behind all the walls of perfection where you need everyone else's approval to be accepted. You are perfected through the Lord above.

God accepts me for who I am because he made me and designed me to be the way I am. Who cares what you think of me? I am me, and you are you, and that is the way it will always be.

Don't try to change me, and I won't try to change you.

It is none of my business what someone else is doing.

What am I doing to make a difference in someone else's life?

Encourage others; build them up on the things that they are good at.

Don't tear them down because they can't do what you can.

Each one of us is blessed with different gifts and talents to share with others.

It helps us not to be in competition with each other but to love each other, as God loves us, just the way we are.

Start today, and respect yourself, and you will be able to respect others in the same way.

Remember everything you do revolves around how you love yourself and respect yourself. It starts with you before things can change. Take a stand; get your self-respect back, and things will begin to change. It will change when and where it needs to be.

The real you—respect yourself—the real you will remain. Be yourself—the real you!

CHAPTER 25

"Be Yourself"

Nothing is perfect, so why do you put yourself through all that agony to be so. You try and try, but it's like leading a dead horse uphill—but you are falling downhill. You put yourself down as you try to keep the notion that you need to be perfect before you get noticed. You find a way to keep going and keep your chin up, and some day it will happen. It is nonsense to put yourself through that, trying to be perfect to be right.

Your kids see what you do, and they think they need to do the same. It is the wrong way of thinking that you need to be raised perfect in a imperfect world. You can't tell your children they need to be raised perfect because nothing's perfect. So take the word perfection right out of your mind and your vocabulary when it comes to anything that isn't so. Let that word go, and see how everything you see will be.

Be yourself, and have fun along the way. Try new and adventurous things you have always wanted to try but never had an opportunity to do. The time is now; why not go for it and reach for the stars? Who knows? You might land on the moon. It is up to you how far you want to go.

What we put in is what we get out of our businesses and in life. Don't let it consume you; let it fuel you when disappointments come your way. Get rid of the old limited mind-set that keeps you frozen in time. Rise up your faith, and get going. Your future awaits you.

Seek God in the morning for direction for the day and what he wants you to do and not do. Get where you need to be so you will able to reach your dreams and your destiny and what he has in store for you that's yet to come. It's already been written for you, as you believe and keep moving forward. Soon you'll see it and feel it as you come closer. You keep on marching into the unknown territory.

The faith and love will help you along the way as you love and release your faith. Go hand in hand as you land. Don't try to get God to do it, but believe and know it will be coming soon. Your breakthrough is coming full speed ahead; live one moment at a time.

Remember what one dream can do—you're unstoppable. Get back in the game of life, and see it through. There is enough room for all of us. Run your race and face all the things you need to face at your own pace. You have the faith to raise the wind.

Changing someone's day might change his or her life.

Believe in yourself. Don't beat yourself up, and focus on all your flaws, and throw fit as you sit. We all have faults and flaws. It's best to admit them and move on from them. You have what someone needs to help change a life. Get up and get going again. No more sitting around and feeling sorry for yourself. All you are doing is defeating yourself in the process over your uniqueness. Why put yourself on someone else's playing field when you have your own playing field to play on?

It is time to celebrate your uniqueness, instead of being afraid to show it.

Get rid of the "poor me" syndrome, the humdrum, and always beating yourself up over the same old same crap from all the years past. Living in the past is trying to live it all over again. You already know the outcome from that. Why do that? You know what to expect, but you are afraid of the unknown. I've done the same radical thing as that. You think it is going to turn out the same as it did before. But putting your trust in the heavenly Father will make a world of a difference. The higher the expectation you put in him, the better the outcome.

Learn to let it go of the past. It has no room in the future, carrying around all that baggage. It slows you down, and you're stuck in the same place for way too long. By trying to carry your whole load of your past, you won't last in the past. You won't know where to go, or what you want to do, or what you had planned for the future in the first place. Let go of what is holding you frozen in time in your past. Always looking in your rearview mirror is fear that is clear. But to be free of it is letting go, and that will bring great cheer as you stand clear of all that fear that appears on the dock.

No more needing to look in the rearview mirror of days gone by. It's a bad habit to stay connected too. A new habit to hang onto is walking and looking forward and focusing on the Lord above. You will see your life change right in front of your eyes. Instead of thinking of the days that have gone by and thinking of the things that have gone wrong, it's best to think of all the things that have gone right. It's the best advice you can give and to take as your own.

First, begin a new dream; and second, push all the past baggage to the curb once and for all. Leave the defeated mentality there as well, the brokenness that you feel inside. God is helping you to let it go, the heart that is cold as steel; Allow your heart to feel once again, so you are able to heal.

Give yourself permission to be yourself and not what others expect you to be.

Being afraid to be outspoken, scared to make a move but standing and not moving anywhere—it takes a moment, and as you take a deep breath and get going again, move boldly and be courageous as you walk down your new path that has been laid out for you. What are you waiting for? Go for it. What is holding you back? Relax, slow down, and read the "fax" God has sent you.

Be still when you need to be. No need to hurry through your life, always in the fast lane. Slow down and savor the minutes you have been given. Enjoy others around you. Help others along the way to bring the best out of them as they bring out the best in you.

In the end, it's up to you how you want to begin.

Your heart will be beating to a new tune; we can do whatever we need to do that God asks us to do. He gives the wisdom and the strength to do whatever he asks us to do. I'm all right for the shape I'm in.

Each day it gets brighter and lighter as I leave all the past in the grass and pebbles that were in my shoes. I leave them and step into a new area that I have never been before. A new adventure is a little scary and nerve-wracking, but it will be worth every moment. Because when I come out, I'll be even stronger that when I went in.

When worry starts to creep in, shake off the worries and be happy.

You have your trust in the Lord; you have nothing to worry about. He has everything covered and under control. Stay in confidence as you begin to dance. Believe, and do not leave. Hold on to your faith; it will see you through. Be confident in what you have been given. So quit telling God what you don't have; appreciate and make the most of what you already have been given.

Time to put your shoulders back and walk with your head up. Don't walk around with your head down in defeat as you look at your feet. You can't see what's ahead of you if your head is pointed to the ground, and you're about to hit a brick wall of destruction, of sadness, of defeat, sitting on your seat without leaving your seat.

We all should be holding our heads up and looking straight ahead for the next adventure to unfold. Keep moving forward in faith and love from above, and keep praising and raising your arms, and thank God for each aspect of your day. God's favor will multiply what you have been given as you keep on living. Don't lose hope; it is coming. Keep on believing and soon you will receive.

Mercy is new for each of us every day. There is always something for us to learn in everything we go through and from all the things we are asked to do and say to others. Keep your faith up, and believe your dream is coming to pass. Be still, even when you feel like running out the door.

Take a moment, and take in the surroundings, and enjoy and savor each moment. You never know when it will be taken from you, and you won't again see that room, and the field of corn running for miles, and flowers flowing in the breeze as you hit your knees.

Showing love and savoring the time with your family may be cut short because our time here on earth is an instant, and that instant might be snapped up in the blink of an eye. Don't take your family and friends for granted, for any rhyme or reason.

The reason or rhyme is not one you should even be thinking about. The best thing is to enjoy the moment you have been given. Make every moment count. Once that moment is gone, it is gone, so make the most of your time.

Make memories, and let go of past regrets and fits and grudges that linger to get them back. It is nonsense to feel that about others and about yourself. All that added baggage should be left at the curb, once and for all.

Put yourself in their shoes. You've done things in your life that haven't been so nice, and you never thought twice. What has been done to another one? So what makes you any different from them? We all have a tendency to think our hurt is different from someone else's hurt. It's not so; it is as equal a hurt. No more wanting to hurt each other to get back at them. It only hurts ourselves in the long run. And we're right back where we once started. full of hurt and resentful by being so hateful and handing out so many hurtful things o others.

The best way is to give it to God, and he will take care of it, once and for all. Let God give you his love. All we do is accept it, and our lives begin to change. As it did for me, he will do for you as well. Share the love with others. It's all about him and what he has done, not what we have done.

Friends and family are what life is all about, sharing love and memories, and having fun, and helping each other. Bring out the best in them, and they will bring out the best in you. Don't share with each other what is wrong with them; that is between them and God. They are fully aware of the wrongs in their lives without being reminded each and every day from others. Focus on God; he shows you the best in all of us and all the rest.

Everything comes full circle, like the circle of love, when you hand it all to him, and put him first in your life. Love touches you where nothing can touch, and it can change a heart that once was as hard as stone. In return, you will receive love; it is like nothing you have ever received. The things you give are above all the rest.

Sacrifice and serve with love in your heart from the start. The power of love and forgiveness changes more than you will ever know until you start doing it. Don't just say the words but live the action out loud. It shows what truly is in your heart by all the love you give from the inside out.

Nothing will change until you are willing to change. Love opens the door as you walk across; it reaches more than you know. You know what changes the world? It's when you love with all your heart.

Being on fire with love of Jesus will begin to spread like wildfire by each of us, if we pick up our crosses and follow him. It will be the best thing you could ever imagine it to be.

Let go of the words that come from your head because it puts conditions on everything to get his way. The heart eliminates conditions on things. The heart of truth is love, and letting the love in changes more, day by day and little by little. It makes a world of a difference, more than you ever know it can, and it will be by the love you are willing to give and share with others. God's love can move mountains, and faith can move the boulders that are in the way of unbelief as you turn over a new leaf.

When you receive his love and accept his love, it will change your life, and you will never be the same. When you chose to walk in love and leave your other life on the dock, know that God is near. There is no reason to fear because he is here to help you share and to spare you of all the agony and pain that you once felt when you thought you were on your own. He has been here the whole time. As the fear and despair kept you down in the dumps with all the lumps and bumps in the road, you took heart.

Let go of all that past despair. Your future is amazing. Keep moving forward; your award is coming. Are you walking in the direction of love? Are you walking in the direction of fear? Fear holds you in the rear and keeps you stuck in one gear, and that is in reverse, back to where it is comfortable and where you've already been miserable, going nowhere, as you look in the rearview mirror at all the things you've done wrong.

John Wayne put it best: "It is dangerous habit to get into, by looking back."

Remember love changes everything; you have nothing to prove by being you. So why do you need to be in the groove for always being rude when you don't get your way, and you end up acting like a fool? That's not love; it's a spoiled-rotten brat.

Walking around angry all the time and always being upset is not right. Your life will spin out of control as you are on the roll of anger and resentment as you live in the basement. We all have things happen to us; you're not the only one who has gotten hurt. We all have, so pray for others who have hurt you because sometime someone might need to pray for you when you've hurt them.

It isn't a one-sided street, we all have things to go through, some big and some not so big, but all of our challenges make us who we are. They make us stronger, because of the things we go through, so why holler as you grow taller? Don't sit around thinking it might have been this way or that way; it doesn't matter. It happened the way; it was supposed to happen the way it did.

We learn and grow from each and everyday…don't stress and second guess.

Nothing of what you could have done could have changed the outcome. It is what it is. Let it go, and move on from it. Open your heart, and let the love in. If you close your heart, you won't be able to receive anything. When you hold on to bitterness and anger, you are a mess—your miracles don't come down to you. It poisons your disposition and your outcome in life until you open your heart and let love in. Then you will begin to see and receive your fill of blessings to download on to you.

Like a computer downloads special messages that come in her import outlet, it is much the same for us. If we have bitterness and anger and all that negative garbage coming in, we are unable to receive any positive input coming in. It gets all blocked up and freezes until we clean it out, and get rid of all that garbage that has been installed.

Clean out all that negative crap in your heart. Forgive and let go of the negative waves in your soul that fuel the anger and bitterness and the fits you throw down the hills as you fall in life when you don't get your way.

It will be an uphill climb, but it will be worth every hill you chose to climb with the good Lord on your side. You have no reason to hide your eyes from the truth; it will set you free to be you—the real you, the one who is less complicated you. Fully bloom right where you are standing and don't deny your true full self.

Every life has a platform.
What we give is what we get in return.
God wants you to be enlightened.

Love brings out the best in all of us.
No love brings out the worst in all of us.
Lessons bring us to where we need to be, onto where we are going.

What roads to go on and things we need to
face on the race to where we are going.
We are on a journey and adventure of a lifetime.
So why not enjoy the road we are on?
That's guided from above.
It's a pathway to heaven, to where we are longing to go.

Who haven't you forgiven that keeps you from living. The only way you will have peace in your heart and feel the joy down in your soul is to forgive. It will release you from the prison where you have been living with anger and resentment. You have been hidden deep inside you; that prison that has kept you frozen in time.

When you let go and open your heart and are able to forgive once and for all, we can dance in the halls, even when you fall. You can stand up once again, even when you make a mistake.

Expression opens your heart and lets the love in, and the joy and peace is released as it takes place. It benefits you more than you ever know to be able to forgive. It shows your character is developed in you, from the heavenly Father living inside your loving heart from the start. Don't be afraid to show the real you. What's in your heart will come out with what you say. If you want things to change, the only way things will change is if you're willing to forgive. Things will begin to change the moment it takes place.

Pray for someone who lives in anger and is upset over things that need to change in his or her life but is not willing to change. That happiness and joy will someday fill hearts with the peace that you felt on the day that you chose to walk in love and give forgiveness where it needs to be done. And in time, you give encouragement to others that Jesus's love for all of us is available for those who want a better life and to be more at peace with themselves and others around them. Living in peace is more relaxing and more rewarding than you have felt in a very long time. Walking around angry and all tied up in knots is much harder letting go, and being set free is easier than you might ever think possible. Letting go is peaceful, and joy will fill your heart. You will be able to relax as the stress and knots are gone. The trust fills you up, and your belief in something new is amazing, something you never thought possible until now.

You still will have tests and trials; it makes us grow, but you do not have to face it alone. Jesus is right beside you, holding your hand every step of your journey home. No more worrying; you have been set free to be a believer. It is a lifesaver, a life-changer, stepping out and finding out for yourself. Put Jesus first in your life, as he did for all of us, way before we were ever born. He took it upon himself, and died on a cross for all of our sins. He shed his blood that was meant for us, but he took our place. He loved us so much he was willing to give up his whole life for us. Why not give up your whole life for him? Be willing to give up, and accept the love he wants to give you. Help him share the love all around. Start by letting go of all your past that still wants to torment you and wants to hold you back. Letting go is easier than holding on to something that happened so long ago. You cannot hold the past and go into the future. There is no room for both. The future awaits you; go for it. No more looking back, only forward. Yesterday ended last night; today we get to begin again.

God has his best for you up ahead. It is waiting for you to start a brand-new day. Forgive and forget your past hurts, so he is unable to plant roots in your soul that leaves a hole. Look at the cross that Jesus carried for all of us and all the hurt he took upon himself for us. The pain was unbearable for any one person to endure, but he did it without any complaint. It was amazing; it's hard for me to wrap my mind around his love for me.

And that is what true love means—to help and love others without complaining. Be a willing servant of the: Lord. Be a willing, living, and loving and caring for the Lord. It is so amazing how your life will be forever changed. Are you willing to give up everything to receive everything? Put Jesus first, in front of everything; that is true love he will show you firsthand. You will be glad you did by letting go of all that pain and strain of trying everything on your own that is draining you of all your energy from all the baggage of yesterday.

Letting go will free you up for new adventures in life.
Be free to be you.

Do onto others that you would have done unto you.
Forgive others, as God has forgiven you.

Get up, and get going again.

If not, your life will pass you by, not letting go of yesterday. You will be missing out on the best part of your life because you were not there to enjoy it.

Being stuck in the past won't last, only years you've lost.

I've had my moments, but I've found that love will see you through to enjoy the new blueprints that are laid out for you. You're able to color in and around all the spaces that need your input. Someone needs to hear what you have to say; even when it makes no sense to you, but it will for someone who hears it.

There is more out of life than you see on the surface around you.

The truth is your hands rise, and we bow our heads. The words we read in red mean more than you think.

All you need to do is believe that what you read is true. As you are living them out, you will see that is so.

Even though life throws you curves, don't take it to heart, even when you are a little fart. We all get tossed in the cart, and we try everything to get out. The only way is through till the end. No one gets a free ride to hide. Facing things makes you stronger as you live longer. No more being a whiner; be a winner as your days go on and on.

For who I am, God made us the way we are for a purpose, to be there for each other, not to bash one another. For him, we're made in his image. We get our worth and value from him, not from what others think and say about us. We are all valuable in his eyes; we're perfectly made. We are all good; he sees the heart and soul of each one of us. Sometimes our behavior isn't perfect, but all the same, he still loves us. It is none of their business what you do; it is between you and God.

All of us are like roaming Peeping Toms, but we all need to get outside of ourselves and look in for a while. We might see something that we like to see, but we need to face our inner truths that we are carrying with us. We usually can see everyone else's flaws and faults and mistakes, but we're not willing to see our own. It doesn't make us any better than anyone else; we have them; we are God's cracked pot that can be used by God in so many ways to show his light through the cracks.

We are all sinners and pretenders in some way or another, wearing masks that we try to hide behind. God is the God of mercy and forgiveness and the favor of magnitude. No reason to hide in the shade of darkness because the light from the heaven above will forever shine in our hearts. He will never leave us or forsake us.

But God has another plan for you. So let go of all the walls you've been hiding behind. Through God's love, he will help you bring them down. Admit and confess your sins, and your walls will start coming down.

You will see your life in a different light, no longer getting upset and falling into someone else's plate, where you have no business being in the first place. We have our own rows left to hoe. Trying to take over and getting into someone else's business leads to a big mess.

Take your mind off what you need to deal with. What is on your plate in the first place will lead to chaos. What really needs to happen is to let go of your emotional baggage. Let it come to rest as you pass the test of all the rules of fools, playing it cool. Why you are sitting on the stool, making all the rules for them to follow?

For the inner peace you want, you first need to face it, admit it. Ask for forgiveness and receive it, and let go of the things that are filling your mind with all sorts of lies. Believe and trust the Lord above; he has everything under control. When he says let it go, then let it go. His promises are faithful; there is no doubt about it. But to believe is to live it, and you will see your life in a different light. Forgive and forget and move on from it, and don't relive it again. Make a decision today to let it go and never relive it again. Close the door of yesterday, and start living in the moment, and enjoy from this day forward. What's in the past needs to stay there, once you have released it from your grasp. God will take care of what has happened to you in the past. He gives you beauty for your ashes. What an awesome trade, not to have to carry that all around with you.

The key to happiness: the decision to be happy! It doesn't matter if others choose not to be happy. If I'm not happy, there is something that I am not seeing here.

What am I afraid of? Why am I blaming? Take a look, and see what you see. No matter what is going on around you, stay focused on what matters most.

The real living is love and giving. Lord, your will be done. Blast everyone with love. Do your best; that's all he asks of all of us. Do what you can do with what you've been given. God will do what you cannot do. When you feel you're lacking, take a look and see what you are not giving.

When you are not giving, you are pretending. You are not receiving. Practice what you preach—all right, do I believe this or not? You will achieve as you receive.

You cannot be on the fence. You are on one side or the other; it can't be both. You are all in, or you are all out. It is your decision, whichever side you want to be on. If you're riding on the fence, you are hiding; you're being deceitful. It's time to decide, or keep hiding and lying and dining. That's no life at all, as you crawl; do what makes you happy, not what makes others happy.

You will be left behind in the end of your life because you gave in to someone else's beliefs. God has a grand plan for all of us. Listen to your heart; it will lead you the right way to go. Be a blessing everywhere you go. Come out of your shell, and be the best you can be—once and for all. No holding back because you're afraid of what others may say or think about you.

When they say words about you, brush it off. It is up to you, Are you going to let a few negative words hold you back from your destiny that God has for you? Your future awaits you. Go for it. God gives you the strength to go forward every step of the way, even when others don't understand. God understands you and what he has planned for you.

The Lord's will will be done. It will be fun and the adventures of a lifetime. Who cares what others think and say about you? The Lord Jesus loves you more than life itself. Do what's in your heart, and stick with it.

Put your life in his hands; he will see it through. Don't worry; it will be okay. When you worry, you think you will not get what you want. But the truth is, you've allowed doubt to fill your mind with things that are not true. The known is uncertain, but faith is for certain. You will see what you truly believe or not. Fear holds you back from your full potential of being the real you.

Why be afraid of being the real you? You have so much to lose by not being the real you.

It holds you in place, and keeps you stuck in a rut with a pit in your gut. When you fear the unknown, your mind fills up with things that may never happen. Let go of all that worry that torments you from the inside out. Be honest say words that you want to say, not empty words that no one knows.

Time to be brave. Let the words spoken be honest and truthful from the inside. Spoken out side, getting out what is real, no matter what comes against you, be real.

Go for it. God is with you every step of the way; he will hold your hand and not let go.

But you have to let go. He will not let you fall. He will hold you up.

Put your trust in him, and let your life truly begin, and you will enjoy everything all the way till the end. We are in this together from start to finish.

Remember God's principle: you need to learn life's lessons through joy and even pain when it hurts and cuts down deep. You want to remain in your seat of defeat, but he wants you to jump to your feet and celebrate because it will be all right. He is here now to rescue you from life's devastation. That's all it takes, as we take long looks at what has already taken place. What can we learn, and what we can take from everything that we have gone through from day one?

The day and time will take us to the next level of our journey in the race of life that we need to face. It is love as you give it; you will see it as you receive it from above. And it changes lives as well as it changes yours. Give love and don't want anything in return. Is true love as natural as kids give it? Don't pretend to love, but give the real thing without wanting anything in return.

They share what is in their hearts. They live it as they give love from the heart. When you truly love, it will show and speak louder than all the words spoken out loud. Loving the Lord and giving from the heart is a start of a new life that has been laid out just for you. Giving love will do the speaking for you, showing God's love through you.

If you know what changes a heart, you will know what will change the world. That is love from the Lord above, through you to the ones you love. The world you are living in, the part of the world that's around you, in your neighborhood, your living room and in the grocery store, wherever you happen to be, that's your part of the world.

When you love, it touches everyone else outside of your world. It starts with one. It touches everywhere else as well, with that first one touch of love.

Be the change you want the world to be.
To see it, you need to live it yourself to be able
to see the change of the world to be.

The more you live out loud, the more you see
things going in the right direction.
Be the change you want the world to be.

Go out and be a blessing everywhere you go.

We learn from our joy and our pain, even when it hurts. Turn
your hatred into love. You will receive what you have been longing
for, and that is love. Living in love will bring your life around. Your
life get brighter and lighter by living in the moment. No more living
in the past because it won't last, only anger and depression by rushing
into the wind.

Move forward and don't live backward where you've already been
there and done that. Let it go and move forward, God gives you mercy
every day. The world needs love. You need love as well, and God
gives it to you. Let your soul receive it. The best gift of all is his love.

The truth is the light in your soul to spread love and joy. That's
been given to you. Don't hide behind your own ride. Stand tall. He
forgave you. Forgive others as he forgave you. Be the real you!

Talk to God; he will lead you and will heal you. He knows what
you have already done. Be the real you; he know the mistakes that
you will make and what you've already done. He wants you to be
the real you, not a pretend version of you that hides behind all the
masks of fears and tears, afraid of the shadows of the darkness of the
clouds that mask the real true colors of who you really are.

It's time to take a stand and speak honestly what is on your heart.
Take time to smell the roses along the way. Be brave as you give a
rave once and for all, and stand up for what you truly believe in. And
that is love. Enjoy the field of flowers, blowing all around in the field
of dreams. Be the real you that you always wanted you to be. You
are special, and don't allow others treat you any different than that.

Dare to be different, free to be you. You have a choice: you can
be held down in one place, or you can make a place for yourself in

this world. You have something to say and something to live for. We all have a purpose in life.

God, enter in my heart, that you've always been and always will be. You are in me and me in you. So no more sitting down and burying my head in the sand.

It's time to take a stand for something, or you will fall for everything.

To share the love in my heart is a start, as the love of the Lord has done for me since day one of my life. I don't want to act like someone else, I chose to be me.

When you feel like thee is no room for love, take another look. As you look, God will show you the pride inside still has you trapped. By letting everything go, God will pull out the rest of your ego. Your head judges everything from A to Z, not how you really are. Take that step forward, and let go of all the negative thoughts that have been told and things that you've heard that are not true and not you. We need to get in agreement with God. You are special in every way possible. Don't allow others to tell you any different than that. You are a special gift from above; you're a child of the Most High.

So don't deny the magic and excitement you feel inside to come out and shine, even when others do. Shake it off. Others are so way off from your true colors. God sees each burning color in your heart that is so beautiful, as your heart is beating bright and showing him great delight without fright. He sees everything about you, from your desires and all your weakness that you have.

When the words of doubt come and you feel the pressure to grumble and complain just because everyone else does; that doesn't mean you need to join in to fit in.

By giving in, it will never end. Unless you begin to take a stand and say no to all that unnecessary grumbling in the rain in the midst of all your pain and complaining of not getting your own way. Stop and say no when those feeling come around your mind. Stand up and say, "No, I believe God is working in my life. I choose to believe and trust he has everything under control."

Each day is a brand-new day to be the real you!

The things you mean to say and do come from the Lord above; no reason to explain them. What is best is to give your best and nothing less.

CHAPTER 26

Lord, It's All about You

It's all about you, that I do
Each and every day, it's not about me.
It's about *you*.
Keep you first in everything.
It will keep me in line, so divine.
For the rest that needs to be done.
To honor you
We work together; we get farther
When we do
Than when we don't; we don't go anywhere.
We stand alone.
No fun, for anyone.
For two, it is for both.
You honor the right one.
Your life begins to shine.
You will know you're on the right path.
You will have peace
And joy that will go around.
Who is near the pier that has great cheer without fear as God steers.
As we honor our heavenly Father
He will take us farther.
And more fun that we see.
What he has done for one

He will do for another.
It takes just one, one more.
Let that one be you!
He will do for another.
His light will shine through.
What he has done for you
He will do for another.
Spread the good news.
His love passes to another and another.
The love is never ending.
It's only the beginning,
That's never ending.
Keep Jesus first in all that you do.
It will show.
All the fun you will have together.
You will never be without.
You will have more than enough to share.
God's way is the right way.
His way is the only way.
Remember to lean on God's understanding, not yours.
Trust and believe and do.
It doesn't make sense to man.
Do it anyway; God's way is the only way.
You have nothing to lose but everything to gain.
Sometimes the hardest things you do in life are
the best thing you will ever achieve.
What's best for you might not be the best thing for everyone else.
God gives us plans and dreams that work out for us.
To achieve as we believe and as you keep
walking and loving toward
Put God first, and all your plans in his hands
Will work together for everyone.
It is all about him and what he has done for all of us.
Share his love, and receive his love.
It is amazing how your life will turn around in a heartbeat.
By giving up everything, you'll receive everything in return.
It's all about him.

CHAPTER 27

Be Yourself

Be yourself, not like someone else.
God never intended you to be like someone else.
He intended you to be you.
No one else but you because no one is better
qualified to be you than you.
Like no one else, be yourself, free to be you.
Don't act like someone else or try to be someone else.
It does not work, and it will never work, no
matter how hard you try; it won't.
Don't compromise to get a rise for a moment;
you will have to keep it up.
If it's not in your heart to do it, or you do not have peace about it
Don't go ahead and do it because you will end
up frustrated and all upset about doing it.
Do what's in your heart; that's what you need to be doing.
Not what everyone else is doing
Or what others are growing to expect you to
do, to keep them happy all the time.
That's not what you are called to do, to be a puppet on a string.
To please everyone; in the meantime you
lose yourself in the process.
And eventually, it will end badly.
It is like a roller-coaster ride without you in mind.

Like trying to juggle a glass of wine and
getting it all over your face.
By not running your own race at your
own pace that you need to face.
Let yourself off the hook and stop being a jerk,
letting others dictate how you are supposed to
live and how you are supposed to act.
Take responsibility for you and not what
others refuse to take responsibility for
And in turn try to pass it over onto you.
Not going to happen, unless you allow it to happen.
It is okay to say no.
Tell the truth and say what's in your heart.
Be yourself, let your hair down, and be your uniquely divine self.
Start dancing around and onward from being all tied up in knots.
By connecting all the dots in the rain, by letting go of all the pain.
To be you, there is only one you.
What I plan to do is be a little spunkier and
more aggressive every step of the way.
You need to come out and shine, once and for all.
You've got what it takes to pull up stakes and stop
being fake; be willing to face the truth.
You have nothing to prove by being you.
God intended us all to be real.
The real you and me that is deep inside of you and me.
To live our lives the way he intended us all
to live, in balance and harmony.
To live and love out loud; and do the best we
can, and he will do what we can't do.
Be yourself and enjoy every day of your life that you've been given.
Don't try to fill someone else's shoes that you're never going to fill.
You have your own shoes to walk in.
Be the real you and be brave enough to walk on the clouds.
He has given you the strength to do it.
You have nothing be afraid of; why are you not living boldly?

He is with you every step of the way, no need to be afraid.
Get out of the boat and walk on the water that is in front of you.
Have faith you will not drown.
Step out and show the real you.
Do it afraid if you have to.
You will be glad you did, because the
nerves that you feel will slip-slide.
Is there confidence that you need to step out and be strong?
Will it lift you to another level, even if it feels wrong?
Your feelings will catch up.
Life is too short for not living out loud.
You have nothing to lose but everything to gain.
By letting go, see your life through God's eyes.
God made me the way I am.
Be yourself, and do your best; that's all he asks.
Believe the best in all, even when you fall.
God will take care of the rest, and trust and believe he loves us all.
Everyone is divine and uniquely made to be the real you.
Don't compromise yourself to be like someone else to fit in.
If you do, you will let yourself down.
Be true to yourself, respect yourself, and love God.
Love yourself and love others as you do yourself.
It reflects how you treat yourself, how you will treat others.
Don't back down from being yourself, just walk away.
Don't be afraid, if you have to, just do it.
Be you!
You will begin to see the real you that's
been buried down deep inside you.
It needs to come out and shine once and for all.
It takes courage not to get discouraged.
Be who you are, a child of God.
Take a stand and be the real you!
Be yourself like no one else.
Dare to be different, free to be yourself.
Free to be you!

CHAPTER 28

Clothes

Clothes on the outside
Don't make the person.
What is on the inside makes the person.
When you put on righteousness, you are
in right standing with God.
No denying that.
Your slumber awaits you.
You will glow.
Today and every day, a friend is a gift
From God—and that is Jesus.
He came down for all of us.
It does not matter what clothes you wear.
He is already there for you.

CHAPTER 29

The Faith

The clothes that you wear shows the faith you have
When you care what people think of your clothes.
Your faith is not strong, when fear and doubt show up.
It clouds your mind, and you want to hide.
Your pride takes you for a ride and blows
everything way out of proportion.
Then your unbelief slips into action.
Doubt and fear appears to twist the truth.
They soon take root and send you through the roof.
Need to cast out all the unbelief in your heart from the start.
Don't believe it.
It's a lie that only wants you to hide.
Anything you will find that does not line up
with God's Word and his promises
Is a lie to keep you confined with one line
that is defined that's not in line.
No matter how big or small, it can be twisted the truth into a lie.
Don't bow down to its deception; you're only
selling yourself out and others; it isn't God.
He doesn't want you to fall down and fail.
He wants you to succeed through every mile of your journey.

Faith

Can move mountains; fear can tear them down
in a heartbeat that will leave you in defeat.
Under the heat of time, your defeat will
keep you down on the ground
When you don't much care what others think about your
clothes you chose to wear. You are moving ground as you
are moving forward, once when you fell into despair.
Your faith is strong.
God shows up alongside you.
Lends you a helping hand; grab hold and do not fold into a mold.
God gives you the strength and the confidence in him.
All the boldness in the world comes from him
When you chose to stand out and not blend in.
God never changes; he stays the same.
Only love, no matter what.
God cares.
When you talk to him about something, it's handled from day one.
In due time you will see it come to pass; we need
to believe and then we will receive it.
Let people say what they are going to say.
It doesn't matter to me; it's none of my business.

Believe

Do your best and nothing less as you confess
And let God take care of the rest.
No matter what you do or say.
Some will like it, and some will not.
As long as you like it yourself, that's all it matters.
Know that you've done your best and lay it all to rest.

Moving forward

Believe that God loves you just the way you are.
He created you to be you, not to be like someone else but you.

Stand tall, stay in faith, and love with your whole heart.
Keep on believing God has everything under control.
Wear what you want, and be yourself, and have fun.

Love Life
You've been given.
Dance when no one is watching, and dance
with God when the music is playing.
Together, hand in hand, that's the way it will always be.

Trust and Believe
As a child,
That's when you will really see
The way it can be, when you chose to believe.
The truth will set you free.

The Faith
You have in him, he will never steer you wrong.
When you put your trust in thee, that's the
way it needs to be, so you can see.

Trust
Where you put your trust, you'll never rust.
That's where it begins, and it never ends.
When you give love every step of the way.
Your life has meaning and purpose.
Keep walking in love.
Wear the clothes you want to wear.
Show love from the inside out that shines in the morning light.
The love you give, you will receive back.
In due time.

Love

Love that's all you need.
Everything else will begin to fall into place.
Give love, it changes lives.
In a heartbeat, when the heat comes it has
changed before you know it.
The light has changed in your life as well.
Once you start giving, the transformation has begun.
Share the love in your heart; that's where it starts
From the beginning until the end!

CHAPTER 30

Celebrate Life

God is great!
He gave you life.
You have so much life to give.
Give the light you see in your heart.
The light you bring.
Bring all you can.
The best you can be.
Know that you did.
Each day put a smile on someone face.
Join in on a laugh or two.
Celebrate life.
God is great!
We have everything to be grateful for.
Enjoy
The life he gave you.
Go ahead and join in with all the fun.
When you don't join in, you will miss out
on so much life has to offer you.
As you join in, all the fun has just begun.
You see life like little children, laughing
and joking and giggling all about.
Sharing love.
Celebrate life.

Let go; don't be so uptight.
Let your hair down—be the real joyful you
That God wants to see in you.
Enjoy life.
Have fun; that's what it's all about.
It will be okay
To celebrate life!

CHAPTER 31

Carnival Ride

Each day is a ride of a lifetime.
Your time is short.
Why not enjoy every minute?
Every minute passes by when you don't jump on.
You are missing your ride of a lifetime.
Your time is short.
When the moment is gone, it is gone.
Start today.
Enjoy your carnival ride
Before it is over
And your rides are all over.
No turning back
To get in line again.
So hop on, and enjoy all the rides
While you have a chance to dance
To ride and enjoy your life's journey.
Carnival ride!
Full of laughter and tears from our quick
rights and our hard left turns.
From one downhill side and down the other side.
With our mountains that we all get to climb in life.
We win some, and we lose some.
But we keep putting smiles on our faces and wipe away the tears.

We keep marching onward.
We've stopped crying the blues, as we pay our dues.
Sit up and take notice when you hear the laughter of little children.
Celebrate life.
Be the real you for to others to enjoy.
You have so much to give.
Give love and the light you'll see
In your heart, you'll bring out the best in each other.
Be the best you can be; that's all you need.
The more you need, it will be there when you need it.
Enjoy your journey, the carnival ride of a lifetime.
No need to hide inside.
Come aboard; it will be fun you never know
Until you're on the ride of a lifetime, and that is your own journey.
It's been designed with you in mind, you will find
Your carnival ride
Enjoy every moment and the actions you take.
It will be a beautiful transformation by every step you take.
The road that the Lord takes you is the one you
need to be on to get to where you need to be.
Where you are at is time of your journey.
So embrace all the avenues he leads you to go down.
It will be the best thing for you.
If you stay where you are, you'll never know how the story
would have been played out. It won't be the same without you.

Go for it. This is your journey, not someone
else's, but yours to enjoy.
The carnival ride of a lifetime!

CHAPTER 32

Choice

Sometimes you have to do what's best for you and
your life, not what's best for everybody else!

The choice is yours to make.

I choose to shine, not to sit behind in my mind that I'm not good
enough.

By listening, you're being denied my destiny that God has planned
for me to enjoy. The best thing to do is hand everything over to God,
and let him be your guide. He has everything that is best for you and
me. You will find peace of mind and joy that will spring into action
when you let go of all that pressure you've put yourself under.

When you choose to shine and not deny, you'll be fine; you're
right in line. Your life will be divine and shining with love in motion
as a devotion, and do it on purpose to love and to shine from the
inside out.

You may like me or not—it's not for me to decide; it's up to you.
Hand it over to the good Lord above. He will make everything just
right. It's time to ask yourself, do you want to sit here one more day
feeling sorry for yourself? Having one more pity party that gets you
nowhere?

I've finally made up my mind. I'm not going to live all upset all
the time for things that others have done or haven't done for me. That

has kept me from living, grieving all the time for all the things that have gone wrong for so long. It's time to live happy and joyful and spread the good news that you've heard and seen. We have no reason to be sad but to be glad for all the things we have; we are so blessed.

The heavenly Father has given us love to share with others for the love he has given us. Ask him to come into your heart; that's a start. Roll the cart; your life will be forever changed; you will never be the same from that day on.

I'm letting you know this happened to me, and it will happen to you as well.

You will find when you let his love in,
it will heal you from within.
The choice is yours; no one will make it for you.
If you want to change, this is the way.
Be willing to let go of the past at last; it will take time.
It will be worth it every moment in time as
you climb and stop denying and lying.
Your future awaits you.
Make the choice!

CHAPTER 33

Things Happen

When things happen to you, what happens to your respect for others? Do you turn your back on them, or do try to be just like them? In other words, do you act like them when they are selfish and mean, or do you try to keep the peace, no matter the cost? The cost might be more than you ever thought possible. At the time, you didn't think you could handle one more little mistake. Sitting back and looking at the mistakes you made are hard lessons learned, and we grow from all of them.

If you never make a mistake, you will never know it until you go through the process. Learning and growing from all the mistakes in life will bring you to where you need to be. Life makes you stronger and bolder as you lean on God's shoulder.

With the stepping stones of life, we will find out how strong we are as we are going through all the growing pains we all go through to be where we are right now. It stretches our faith and our hope in new adventures up ahead to where we are going.

Keep looking forward, and let go of what lies behind. Don't relive your past dreams and all the past hurts on your shirt carry around all that guilt.We are not made that way. We are to learn as we go, and keep marching forward, and keep our focus on Jesus. He will guide us every step of the way. We're not here by ourselves; he is here every step of the way home.

Live out your dreams and enjoy all that life has in store for all of us. We may endure some things that we were not prepared for. Through our tests and trials, some are hard and some are easy. You'll never know until you're in the midst of one. How you handle your ups and downs is what you need to learn, and it gets burned in your attitude. That sometimes needs a little improving, and it does over time. Soon you will grab onto it, and sometimes it takes a lot longer that you thought.

To get in agreement with God, he shows you what part you need to work on. When you try to handle things on your own, before you call out to God, it turns into a big mess before you confess. You go up for recess as you begin to stress that you need God's help as you cry out. God comes and intervenes as you lean on him. He makes everything right once again.

If I would wait for his guidance and his direction, instead of my own nonsense, it would go much smoother, once I got a hold of it. Sit back and put your trust in Jesus. He has already been where we have been, so he knows what we are going through and where we have been. He is not surprised at what we do.

You have no need to beat yourself up on things you do or say. Each day is a day of learning. We learn something new each and every day. Even though you don't know at the time, you're learning and growing every step of the way. No matter how old you are pr how young you are, we learn from each other.

The young teach the old, and the old teach the young. It all comes full circle in the end. What you learned when you were young you take forth with you when you are old. The things you share with the young help them to not make the same mistakes that you once made. Some chose to learn the hard way on their own. You can't complain about that because you were once in their shoes, wanting to explore the unknown on your own as our kids are doing right now. Learning by experience makes us stronger and wiser. That makes us who we are today.

By sitting and going over things in your mind that have brought you to where you are today, sometimes you want to cry, and sometimes you want to laugh until tears are streaming down your cheeks. We all have to do that every now and then; it helps us get rid of all the negative activity going on in our minds. It helps us look at life and appreciate all we have been given, instead of all that we are missing, all the things we think we are missing out on. Realistically, we need to enjoy all that we have been given, not what we think we deserve but what we are supposed to have.

If we are supposed to have it, we will have it, and if not, we will not. God always has our best interests in mind for us. Things happen, and things don't stay the same, even though it's hard when things change but you want them to remain the same. The more you're in pain, the more you want it to disappear. Claim it and move on from it, or you will remain the same. That's how life goes on. It doesn't stand still, even though we stand still, and we chose to remain in one space because we are afraid of change. It is time to step forward, or you might get run over.

By always looking over your shoulder, trying to figure out all the unanswered questions of why things happened the way they did, you won't find out that way, living in the past and lifting up all the rocks that have been laid down on your path through life. You can't change the past, but you learn from it, and go onward and grow from there. Your future awaits you to enjoy a new path that is up ahead. Let go of all the past trips of trying to figure everything out for the answer you need.

The free you will become to be the real you, not following all the rules you've put on yourself. We all have flaws; we all need to accept that we do. Free is always better than following all the rules, acting like fools to be like everyone around you, to fit in the clique. Being in the cliques is so overrated, and that is not for you. The real you that God intended you to be is unique and divinely designed. We all need to loosen up and not be so uptight, like an overwound wristwatch.

Life has put us on a fast track to nowhere fast, always up tight to get everything done, all in one day. By going so fast all the time, you never get anything done. Try it sometime—slow down and see how much you get done. You will be amazed what you get done, more than you could ever imagine. Plus, you're not in a rush, and you don't miss a thing throughout the day. In our fast-paced world, everyone thinks more is better, but reality is less is better. Slower makes you closer.

You can't enjoy what you already have been given when you are ready for the next exciting thing to come along, so you can belong in the group. When everything you do and see is exciting, no matter how big or small, you will be content and appreciate what you have already been given. You life passes by so quickly by living so fast. You don't enjoy it as you run through it. By running and running, soon you will run into a brick wall, and it will bring you to a standstill. You wonder what happened, where your life has gone. Your kids have grown and moved away, and you're left alone pondering all the things you have gone through, now they are gone.

What do you know, now that they are gone? You really didn't live and enjoy your life, because you ran through it as you endured life's challenges each and every day. That was yesterday, and yesterday is gone. But today is today, a brand-new day to begin again. We need to let go of yesterday's wine and grab hold of the wine of today to enjoy as we take a sip. Things happen, and things don't remain the same for a reason, and the reason we don't know is that we don't need to know. We know as we go.

When the time is right, we will know, but for now, we need to move forward and enjoy the moment we are in. Life goes on; we learn from all the trials and tests as we confess. The stepping stones of life bring us to where we are right now.

We trip and we fall; we get up and get going again. For the next curve and the bump in our roads make us stronger as we live longer. We change each passing day as we grow older and wiser through are experiences that we endure. The heart and soul gets softer as we become calmer and stand tall as we listen to our hearts. Share your life with others as you walk through it. Don't be afraid of the rain and all the pain you go through; it makes you who you are. God intended that we be more like him.

Be the real you, not some pretend phony full of complaints and grumping remarks. It is the life he has planned for each one of us, blessed in so many ways. We need to grab hold of his hand. Life is to be fun and to be the real you. Be bold and confident in Jesus; he will show you the way.

Give love and receive love back in return.
You get what you give!
Things happen; you don't need to be frozen in time.
Learn from it and move forward; don't be stuck in reverse.
Your future awaits you; leave your past in the past at last.
Enjoy the moments you have been given; it's a gift.
You don't know what tomorrow holds in store,
but you know the moment you are in.
Savor every moment as a memory to remember.
Remember things happen.

Chapter 34

Meaning

The meaning of the things we do and the things we say.
Are from the choices we make; do we make
the right ones or the wrong ones?
The way we know if they are or are not the results down the road
Is if we are satisfied with the results; then
you'll know it was the right one.

As I sit and write, it is a great choice to put down on paper what is written on my heart to share with you and others who need to hear what is said. We all know that life throws us curves, the ones that are not expected at all. But it happens; when it does, we pick up and go on. Life's sweets, treats, and defeats we all endure throughout life. Our stepping stones build our character throughout life's long journey.

Don't sit and overthink things that happen. Just know it did happen. When you find out you've made a wrong choice, let go and move on from it. Just remember it is a learning curve. The next day is a brand-new day to begin again. Start all over again, even though yesterday a tornado ransacked your life. It has already happened; there is nothing you can do to change it.

Yesterday ended last night. Don't focus on yesterday today. If you try to relive yesterday today, it will drive you nuts, trying to fix something that has already happened.

It's best to let it be, let it go, and move on from it. You will grow from it and learn. Each day is a learning day. The past is the past, and we can't change that fact. It is best to let it rest in the dust. Grab onto the here and now, and move forward toward the future; see where it takes you. You already lived the past, and you already saw where it has taken you and what you needed to learn from it. Onward toward the future; it awaits you.

The bright light of the new day is upon you. Don't waste it away over things that have already happened. Enjoy every moment that's been given to you; it's a gift from above. No more crying over all the things that have gone wrong in your life. Talk about all the things that have gone right, the blessings you have been given, not the prisons where you've been living but your new beginning away from sinning, with Jesus. He has brought you out of all the bondage you were in, way over your head.

Today is a brand-new day and a brand-new you. Enjoy your life you've been given and start living; you're in heaven. Free to be you. We all have dark clouds above our heads, but they don't have to stay there.

The light shining bright in our hearts tonight
needs to come out and shine.
Don't be afraid to show the real you.
With courage and boldness, it will speak
louder than any words you can say.

Have fun with your family and friends. The memories you make today will last a lifetime. Take some time to get to know them. In your heart, you will be glad you did, as joy fills in all the cracks and the peace remains, where there once was pain. Dreams of the future are up ahead; no more looking back. Of the mess that once was, let it go and keep looking forward. Our reward is up ahead.

The best is yet to come—more blessings are being poured out for you. It's not over until it is over. Keep reaching and dreaming; the vision is so big. You're a part of the big picture of which we are all a part, even when you don't think you are. But you are.

Listen to your inner guidance; it will lead you where to go. Ask Jesus to come into your life and be your Savior. Ask him for forgiveness, and repent. He will and he will move in and never leave you or forsake you. He will be with you every step of the way. Your life will be forever changed. You will still have tests and trials, but you'll have Jesus on your side to help you grow through them.

You are right where you need to be. Be patient; it will be revealed to you in due time what is next for you to do, but in the meantime, keep doing what he has placed in your heart to do. Be a blessing, and keep growing where you have been planted.

Encourage others to do the same, to go out do your best. It shows in all that you do. The light shines bright in your heart tonight. It will be all right, even when there are clouds all about. Remember the sun will always come out sooner or later; it always does. The outcome is better than the day before the clouds came out, and gloomy days are no more. We have no reason to mope around to have a gloomier day.

Now that we have Jesus in it; our lives get brighter and much lighter than ever before. He brings out the best in all of us with the light he brings into the dark world. And the love he shares with all of us. Keep looking up when you feel like going downward. Moving forward, our steps get lighter and brighter with every passing day.

Put a change in your mind, and look toward the heavens, and the light in your heart will get brighter and brighter. The joy fills up and flows over the edges of your heart.

Live out loud with love in your heart, and share the love that is buried down deep in your soul. Love speaks louder than words, and the actions you take will do the speaking for you.

Make the choice today that you will be happy down the road from here.

Mean what you say, and do what you say. Your belief in your heart will show in your actions. It builds your character, one word and one action at a time. One word can build someone up and also tear the person down in one instant. Love stands strong by the actions we choose to take and not fake, for someone else's sake. Tell the truth; it is the root to all who care and love you from the start.

It says a lot to what we believe; what we think shows what we believe. The truth is we need to trust Jesus more than what our minds think. It's not what we know; it who we know, and that is Jesus and what he has done, more so than what we've done and accomplished. Our minds get us so confused with what we should or shouldn't do. You need to do what's in your heart, and your feelings and mind will catch up to your heart.

Believe and put your trust in God. He has your best interest in mind. Love and forgive; it will help you every step of the way. Treat others the way you want to be treated.

All we need to do is believe. And you will begin to see.
The light of day forever more.

Keep moving forward and love all along, and you cannot go wrong. Help others to believe their future is bright, and they will not need a flashlight. It will be as bright as day, flowing sunlight shining over the mountaintops. As you help others, you can see their smiles and the light glowing all around for miles over the horizon.

Light a spark in people's hearts that will last a lifetime by seeing their potential—what they can be when you believe in them. Soon they will be able to see it themselves as love takes root in them. It will begin to show by those encouraging words spoken over their hearts that once were broken.

Light those sparks in someone else, as someone did for you. Show love and honor and respect others; be a blessing to everyone. It can grow with one glance as you give someone a chance with a positive and encouraging word.

The outlook on their lives is amazing with all the love you can share, as Jesus has done for you forever more. What is up ahead of them? All the dreams and the visions you can paint that is so bright for them. Don't get discouraged, even when things are not going just right for you.

Remember this too shall pass. The light will always come out tomorrow, even when the sun isn't out today. Your future shines bright when you focus forward and let go of the past.

Show love; it spreads like wildflowers flowing in the breeze. It will never freeze as long as it flows through you to another. It will back up in you, though, when you stop giving love. Love is amazing to give to another who doesn't expect it. It does the most to who receive it and who give it, and you will receive it. It comes full circle and touches as it changes.

Chapter 35

"Things Happen."

When they do, what do you do?

Why sit and ponder what has happened? Why not get up and do something amazing? You get up and take that first step and do something bold, and then God shows up and opens the doors that need to be open and closes the doors that need to be closed.

Your whole life is a journey to enjoy every moment. It can be taken away in a heartbeat; just as it has been given, it can be taken away. Don't take one moment for granted or the people in it; they can be here one moment and gone in another.

Your family, your friends, your kids—enjoy the laugher, the giggling, having fun with each other. Throw the angry words and thoughts right out the window. It's not worth throwing them at each other; it's for the birds.

All the cussing and fussing and being all tied up in knots—it's best to let it go and move on from the mistakes and all the rakes and fakes of the past. The past is the past; why even go there? Nothing can be changed by the words and thoughts of the past.

The best thing you can do is to leave it in the past.

Start a new day and begin again.
A fresh start in the morning, we are given each day.
The light in the morning dew makes it all better.

If your day starts out dark, it doesn't need to stay that way.

Start with looking around, and see what's around you.

The beautiful sunset and birds flying all about and singing has been given to us to enjoy. Why not take time out of your busy day to enjoy the splendor of God's glory?

The light shines in our hearts when we take time to do the things we love and do what we love. If you don't like what you doing, it's time for a cool change.

As we take that first step, we go forward. The darkness starts to lift from your heart and light fills us up with joy. The real you starts to appear, and the old you disappears as a distant memory. It comes back when you fall backward into your old patterns of living.

When the darkness tries to reappear and pull you back down in the old pain once again, when things get tough, say no, and don't give in but dig in. You have what it takes to move onward. This feeling only lasts a little while and then moves on. Live beyond your feelings and the old negative voices in your head. The negative waves are only waves that come, and it's best to let them go right out the window of your heart.

The same old voices grow old after a while when you walk around with no smile. Everything remains the same when you walk around holding on to you old pain in the rain; it leaves a stain on your heart.

Make a new start with a new heart; let go of all the negative thoughts that keep you held down to one spot. With the darkness you see in your heart, it's time to fill it with the light. Speak positive words over you that God has given to speak over your life. That will make a world of a difference in you outer appearance. It will be written all over your face. Where darkness was, light has taken its place.

You were holding your last piece of rope, and you thought you had no hope; you wanted to jump and take yourself out of the equation. There is always another option and that is to call out to Jesus; he has been there. He knows what you are going through.

In your mind, you hear all these thoughts where you want to escape all the pain you've been feeling. You sit and throw fits, and you begin to sink into a pit of despair and darkness, where you thought the only way out was to go away and never come back again—in other words, to take your own life and be done with all your pain, And your mind says that needs to be done.

Don't listen to your head; it will steer you wrong!
You are special in every way possible.
You are needed in this world; you're part of God's wonderful plan.

Your head plays a recording over and over that doesn't make any sense. There is one thing for sure: Jesus is your only way out. He will help you through and get you out of your pit of distraction and destruction. Through his help, you will come out better than you ever thought possible. Jesus knows what you are going through when others turned their backs on you. He knows because that happened to him, when his friends turned their backs on him.

So if you think taking your life is the answer to all your prayers, think again. Jesus is the answer to all your prayers, to all that you've been going through. You don't have to face it alone. He will help you through. Awesome news; you don't have to go through life alone. He is here to help us, whatever life throws us, good things as well as the not so good things. It is hard to take in, that there is someone who cares for us so much he would die for you and me. Who do you trust—your head or your heart?

I've been right where you are standing right now—on the fence where you are right now. Should I stay or should I go? The choice is yours on whom to believe. Why not take a leap of faith and believe in something that will take you farther than your wildest dreams?

The path you are on right now only leads to darker and darker living in park, which will only hurt you and take you far, far way. When you choose the darkness, your mind fills you up with turmoil with pills and drills that kill. With destruction and devastation, it mounts up to a state of confusion and takes you far away from your family and friends who love you.

Others may hurt you, but by your leaving in that fashion, you will leave a big hole that only you can fill. We all need what you have to give. I know life is hard, but we don't mean to hurt you. Sometimes we do; please don't take it to heart. But forgive me, and let me love you again—God's way, with no strings attached.

Unconditional love says more than anything.

When others hurt us, give it to God; he will take care of it for you.

Remember he's our vindicator, our deliverer of all things. We don't need to chase them down and take revenge; he has it all covered. Pray to God to give you the strength to forgive and move on from all the hurt. He has a grand plan for you, even when others try to get you discouraged and distracted by keeping you down when they are down in the dumps themselves. We don't need to allow the hurtful words to fill us up.

Don't give in to that negative rigmarole that tries to get you upset. It's a waste of time to let it get under your skin. It takes your focus off God's plan for your life.

Depend on Jesus every step of the way, and let go of all the past hurts. You've got what it takes to reach your dreams, even thought others don't understand. He does grab hold of your hand and take a stand where you land. Your future is with him in the end. He brings you new friends as the old ones fall away, and that is okay. Everything comes full circle in the end, so no reason to pretend.

The sunshine comes out after the darkness starts to fade in the rain of all that pain. The flowers will bloom once again, even when it is gloomy and a storm starts to form.

We grow and learn from the storms that start to form.

A heart has a light, and it burns bright in the morning light,
Even when the clouds are floating all
about as the sun shines through.

When things happen, don't camp out on them. Let them go and grow and learn from the experience.

Live lives full of light shining bright in our hearts tonight.
God has a plan for all of us, so don't lose sight of that.

Even when storms come, and you don't see the light, know it is there, as you're in the storm. Remember the sunshine will come out once again. Move onward after the storm passes and fades in the night. A distant memory, a few clouds remain as the sun shines through the cracks of your past. That is okay to share the love with others and your story of the darkness of years past. And know it will not last.

The storm has passed and the darkness fades into a distant memory to go onward.

Even when things happen,
We learn and go on from there!

CHAPTER 36

Friendship

What is a friend to you? Are you a friend?
Being a friend is more than just knowing their name.
But what's in their heart. That's a start.
Getting to really know them, a real
relationship, that's what life is about.
Learn by hearing.
The eyes tell a story if you are willing to truly listen.

Open your heart as the story unfolds.

As they begin to speak, one word at a time. What's on their heart as the days go by? You can learn a lot by listening and really hearing what they are saying, what they've been through to make them act the way they do.

Don't judge by what others say and do or the way they dress, or you will begin to act like you know best. In fact, you don't know what's best at all. And you will begin to fall in the hall and take a spill yourself. So don't laugh; it could be you. But through the grace and mercy of the good Lord above, you could be standing there yourself.

How someone dresses doesn't make the man or woman. It's what is inside that really counts, more than how they dress. It is more important how you treat people than what you do for them, because if you don't treat them right, whatever you do for them won't make a difference. By treating them right, whatever you do for them will change their world.

How you treat someone behind closed doors should be as important as when your friends are watching. It shows how much you really care, and your character is revealed.

The fruit of people's hearts shows up when the heat is turned up on high. How they act when the rug is pulled out from underneath them. The truth is revealed, where their hearts are when they don't get there way.

What you say and do and the actions you take when you make a mistake, or, better yet, when others make them, as well how you handle it when it is your friend who makes the mistake—do you stand and let it go, or do you run off with an angry attitude when you don't get your way? Face it; we all get angry, but the anger can consume us if we take it out on everyone in sight.

The best thing is to let it go and move on from it, even if it doesn't make sense. The actions you take shows what is in your heart and is where it will always be. It is good for all of us not to get our way every time. Sometimes we win and sometimes we lose, but remember we are truly blessed. We grow from both, even when it hurts sometimes. We still go on, even when it still hurts inside.

Just think about it: if we got our way all the time, we would act like spoiled brats. Then when you didn't get your way, after you have grown accustomed to getting it, it would be worse than you think right now. How boring life would be like if we acted the same and always got our way.

Learning to trust and believe and then receive is a more peaceful way to do things. It's awesome how God has it all worked out, and that is the way it needs to be, to be grateful and thankful for what we've been given and stop pretending that we're not. When we truly are, then we need to say so, and believe God has our best interest in mind, so why deny? Simply believe and trust. Know he is working behind the scenes, and your breakthrough is coming through soon. It is coming; wait with a good attitude.

Some days things go your way, and some days they don't. It shows a lot on the days you don't get your way. The best thing to do is to let it go and move on from it. If not, you'll be holding on to it for a long time by camping there. It will hold you back from giving your best and leaving the rest up to God.

By holding a grudge, you are unable to love. By letting go, you will enjoy the grand plan God has for you. The fruit of love you walk in, the love you leave behind as you walk by is how you will be remembered long after you're gone.

A friendship means a lot as you stop and share your story with others along the way. By telling others you care and showing them how much you care, it speaks louder than words.

Having good friends is being a good one first.
What you can do for someone else is more important.
Do it out of love, not what you can get from them.
But what you can do for them
Will show what's really in your heart right from the start.
By doing some things first, lead by example;
it will show the real you.
What a good friend you are.
By walking and talking the talk.
You walk the walk right down the sidewalk.
Be a good friend.
Lead by example.
Be a good friend, and stick like glue, and
be the best you that you can be.
Go out of your way to be a person of excellence,
and don't be embarrassed; just be you.
Jesus leads by example; look and see how you will be.
He wasn't afraid to help; he did it out of love
for you and me, and he was just himself.
Walked and talked his love out, one step at a time.
Be the friend you want to see
As Jesus is a friend for each of us.
Be a friend.
It starts with you and me.

CHAPTER 37

A Story of Trust

When you think everything is running smoothly, you think nothing can go wrong or will go wrong. Life happens, and you wake up to things that begin to happen. You think things wouldn't happen, but they happen. Those are growing pains and stepping stones that take you a quick stage left.

The morning news is about something getting canceled and trying to understand why; then making phone calls, trying to figure out why. That time was right, and then you will know the answer why. At the same time, you get another phone call and get yelled at about something that you had no control over. No matter what you said, it couldn't make a difference anyway.

When someone is on the warpath about something, you can never make them happy. Trying to make an unhappy person happy is a never-ending battle.

I found out that day where my priorities lay, take it or let it go. That day I let it go and listened to my little voice inside, and hung up the phone. That's exactly what I did; no one has the right to talk to someone in that matter, no matter who they are. That includes me as well, talking in that tone. Nothing in life is that upsetting to go off on other people. The best thing anyone can do is to leave them talking to themselves and be mad all by themselves.

It was the day I started to let things go. I still have a long way to go, but I was on my way for change, not letting people run over me and take advantage any longer or by trying to keep everyone happy, when they have clearly chosen to be unhappy. That is their choice to be unhappy, but it isn't my problem to make them happy.

We all have our own jobs to do, but keeping everyone happy isn't one of them.

Encourage them and be nice to them. Help them when they need something; that is one thing. But trying to please everyone all the time is wrong. No matter how hard you try, it will never be good enough. Do your best, and let go of the rest. There comes a time in your life when enough is enough; others need to take a stand in their own lives. We can't do it all for them. It's time for them to begin trying things on their own.

Time to set boundaries. There is a time to say yes and a time to say no.

When you know it becomes too much, it is time to change. If you don't make a change, it will keep going on and on until you are broken, and you can no longer be there. You will fade away, and no one will really care because you never set boundaries for yourself. Once you set them, follow through with them.

You were pleasing everyone else and afraid of upsetting the apple cart, and had a fear of rejection by saying no. In the long run, you don't respect yourself by not saying no and enough is enough. By waiting, it will get way out of hand. Then it will be almost too late to make a change.

In the beginning, change is hard to face, but the way to get going is to get moving. To get respect is to start giving it first, and treat others with the same respect. Be direct and to the point. Be honest or you cannot rest. Say yes when you mean yes, and when you mean no, say no. You will begin to see what happens firsthand and what is really important.

It's not who is always right and who's always wrong, but how we can all get along, to live in peace and harmony for the rest of our lives as we confess. What really matters most is to be there for others who need us.

My priorities were focused on the wrong things. I always was trying to put others' fires out but was unable to face my own—until my life was shaken, and I was brought down from the clouds where I was living. No matter what you do, you can never make someone happy if the person doesn't want to be happy in the first place. Our best thing is to do our best and be nice, even if others are not nice. But know that you were nice.

If they choose not to be, let go and hang up—how freeing it was. Don't be controlled by others who have no intention of ever being nice but only want to bully you and control you until they get what they want, and then they will not be happy. It is a never-ending battle that we all go through, even the things that we receive. Without a grateful and thankful heart, we are all in the same boat.

Move on and put your focus onto things that really matter, and let go of the things that don't matter at all. Even when the small stuff seems a little rough, it is tough letting go of the little things you cannot change.

Help the ones who need your help, and let go of the ones who refuse the help. So that is what I did—put my focus on something that was more important than life itself.

I put my trust in the Lord, and let him guide and direct me. Sometimes I still struggle. That day, God spoke to me and said, *"That little boy needs your help right now; tomorrow maybe too late."* It's time to delegate as you congregate. Let go of always trying to put others' fires out. Do what you can do, and let God take care of the rest.

The other fire that you were trying to put out will go out on its own.

God shows you things by allowing things to happen that are out of your control. It shows you that things happen, and you can't always put the fire out. I can only put out no doubt. But believe and you will receive.

To make you realize where your priorities lie, stop and look around at all the gifts you've been given. Listen to what is going on around you; it isn't right. Stop doing what you've been doing, Help is needed. Has it found you? It's right in front of you.

The blessings are upon you. The story is at hand for you to read that you've been living. You're still here to tell. Your eyes are wide open to see from the beginning to the end of the story. Listen and see.

Everything seemed like a fairy tale, going so fast, relying on money and yourself, that something was about to go wrong in your fairy tale world. The caring for others went right out the window. It begins as one for all and all for one. What started out as meant for good turned right in the middle. Too much of a good thing can turn bad in a real big hurry. It was bound to happen, sooner or later.

It's like riding a bicycle ninety miles an hour when the chain breaks. We all need a wake-up call. We've been living far too long with our eyes closed. Sometime things are allowed to happen, to do that everything.

When the chain broke, it brought you to your knees, which was bound to happen sooner or later. Remember later always comes when you least expect it, but it does, when you are living in this fast-paced world we all have been living.

We get our priorities all mixed up as to what is really important. To love others, put their needs above our own. Instead, we are taking care of our own needs, not helping others or even wanting to talk to anyone at all. We only help to get from them. We all need God to make things right again and to be willing to help a friend. He will help you get your priorities right in line with his.

It takes us all to sit up and take notice, and own up to our own actions and fake along the way. No more blaming and shaming. It's time to take responsibility for our actions. We all have a part to play in God's plan for our lives. He gives us the free will to make choices each day.

The consequences of the choices today will show up tomorrow, so we need to make wise ones so we will be happy with tomorrow, and our conscience will be at peace from the start.

Everything happens for a reason, some good and some bad. W we can learn from them all. It's here to help us, not to hurt us. The reason you don't know at the time is because it will teach us something down the road; that is going to take place and we need to face the way things happen the way they do. It time, things will become clear; that is why things happen the way they do.

The true test of trust comes into play. Who and what are you putting your trust in? Your trust needs to be put into place first. Don't wait until it is your last option. It happens that way when we put our trust in ourselves to fix it all on our own, where we think we are smarter than God—that's a disaster waiting to happen.

When life slowly throws a cog into the chains of our bicycles, it gets harder and harder to peddle uphill. With the brake on, it's like dragging all your baggage up the hill, thinking you don't need help, that you have it all handled. But the truth is, God is allowing things to happen to reach you, since nothing else will but this. A wake-up call, you are unable to make it on your own without his help.

It happens in such a way when we put our
trust in ourselves to fix it on our own.

When something is taken away, it is best to let it go and not to worry about why, just know it had to be this way. Even though it was a blow to all of us, God allowed it to happen. We in trusted in ourselves and not in him. Where it needs to be, he is here to help us.

The world system is that you do everything yourself, or it will never get done. You get angry and upset when things don't go your way. You think it needs to be a certain way to be right. But your way isn't always the best way.

The things needed to change to go in the other direction; we were going the wrong way. We grow and know we needed to change and put our trust in God that he will make everything all right once again. It doesn't happen overnight, but it doesn't do anyone any good if we are walking around angry all the time.

What does it do? Nothing at all. When you try to take things into your own hands and fix them, it will only get you frustrated and upset, Until you stop and hit your knees and ask for help, you will never get anywhere, only despair. You will keep going around the same mountain like you always have. Peddling like you are on a bicycle, going around and around, and you're not going anywhere. You will be in the same spot that you are right now.

Talk to God; he has all the answers to your situations. The solution is one prayer away. Why try to get all the answers on your own when he's there for the asking? All things are possible when you put your trust in the Father above. When you do, the next morning is always brighter than the day before. The answer is there for you that wasn't there the day before. The light came on in the night, and the answer was given.

When you are stuck on something, you need a good night's sleep, and the answer will be there in the morning light. Life hasn't been easy, but persevere onward. Is the reward to do your best, and God will do the rest? We are partners with God; we work together like a well-oiled machine.

Know you did your best; don't compromise your life to fit in.

When someone asks you to do something to fit in, the best thing for you to do is walk away and not look back.

Trust God; he will send someone new in your life
Who will love you for who you are.
Keep moving forward with your cards at
hand; be yourself, the real you.
The unique and divine self; it will mean the pressure is off.

When you are who you are supposed to be, the
real you, not someone you pretend to be.

Trust God in everything; it is the best you see indeed, plant a seed.
He knows what is best for all of us.
Trust God with all your heart!
That is a start you will see in your heart.
Your life will take on a new look and color for you to see.
Put your trust in the one who has your best interest in mind.
Trust God with all your heart and soul.

Chapter 38

Change Takes Action

Change takes action with no distraction.
God gives you the strength you need to do what you need to do.
Believe it and receive it.
It is true for you and for me.
Go for it; what do you have to lose? You have everything to gain
By moving forward; don't be left behind in
the wind because you were afraid.

Your future awaits you. If you stay here, you will always be in the rear, full of fear right here. Change takes action with a plan. Without a plan, it doesn't work.

Embrace the change, the change in which you will see your dreams come to pass. Every step you take, you grasp the way that it is leading you to where you need to go. Even though the world thinks you need to be perfect to be beautiful, it isn't so. The true beauty is deep inside you. It comes out slowly as you take action; you'll see over time.

You don't have to be perfect to be you.

Put your trust in the Lord above; he will guide you every step of the way. It is up to you to decide what is right for you. Let others think what they are going to think. You are going to do what you are going to do. It will be what it will be to be me. It's time to be brave and honestly say what I want to say.

Lord, I have not the time or the energy to get everyone to like me, so I give it to you. It's none of my business what others chose to think of me. Stand up for myself, or I will not stand up for anyone else when it is time. The time is now; no more bowing down to someone else's level that brings the devil out of me.

Take a stand so you will land to where you need to be.

Say to yourself out loud, "I accept myself. I love myself. I know I have weaknesses and imperfections, but I will not let them stop me, and I will not allow them to stop God from working through me as he changes me to be what I'm supposed to be." Doing this several times a day, soon you will develop a new attitude toward yourself, a new outlook on life and a greater level of confidence in God. My heart deeply rejoices.

Who cares what others think and say about you? I'm going to be a diamond some day. You're on your way, a work in progress, every step of the way. Don't listen to negative words and false accusations about you; it is just trying to get under your skin to get in, to keep you from God's best for your life; the plan that is so defined that is in line with his will for you.

You are special, and so are others. Show others the blessings that are in your heart to share with others, even when they are grouchy and mean and make a big scene. Give mercy to all who get under your craw, and all you want to do is sit and bawl and call and fall to the ground.

What are you doing to make someone else's life special? We are special in our own and wonderful ways. God has made us unique in every way possible. See what is in someone's heart, and what the person can be; the future you will see indeed.

The way they act right now isn't their best that you can see in them. Help bring out the best in others, and they will bring out the best in you, the positive attitude you have toward others. In turn, you will have a positive outlook on life. When you choose to live in a more positive way and take the focus off "what about me?"

Put your focus on making a difference in someone else's life, being a part of the big picture. When you put your mind to it, you can do it. When you focus on helping others, God will send someone to help you. You see, he has everything under control. Give someone else chances, helping them reach their full potential. Don't focus on the money—what you can make off one another. Focus on how you can help them with what they need indeed. Is what we all need indeed not to be full of greed and get more than we all need? And then want more and more.

You are never satisfied until you let go of "what about me?" and "what can you do for me?" Nothing is going to change unless you are willing to change and take your mind off yourself and what can others do for you.

You want to be part of the change you want to see.

It will start the moment you ask yourself and God, "What can I do for others that you've done for me that I didn't deserve, but you loved me anyway?" Take action; you can do it one action at a time to help someone in need.

Our imperfections will not stop God from working through us unless we let them. We need to accept ourselves completely, our weaknesses and messes and all, because God does. He made us the way we are because we need him every way possible. Remember—God looks at our hearts. Don't let your weaknesses stop you.

Be determined to let God work through you in spite of them. The change he knows needs to be done in you. With each step you take, the change is happening in you more than you know, but it is better each day and with each step you take.

When you think it, you will speak it. So if something comes into your mind that isn't every nice, don't think it. Cast it away, and start thinking of something nice instead.

It helps others, though, the kindness that you give, more than angry words spoken out of turn. You never know what is going on in someone's world.

The grace you give today will help someone
down the road by the road you take today.

There is always a road to take: the wide one everyone else is on, or you can get on the narrow path that leads you down the lightened path that God has laid out for you to follow.

To lead you home to him.

Help others see the path where he is leading you, by the way you live and all the things you do and say, the kindness and mercy you give as God gave it to you. Share it with others. The action you take today will see the results down the road.

The change and the results are better than ever before.

We grow by the changes we make and the old habits we break. Replace with new habits that take us to new levels to grow and learn from them. Each and every day we learn something new that changes our outlook on life. That helps us to help others in the process. Your pain is someone else's gain, even in the rain.

The changes and actions we choose to take
will make a world of difference.

By the actions we chose to take, others may doubt what we say, but they see what we do. It shows what is in our hearts when we chose to live love out loud in everything we choose to do.

Even when they have hard things to face, it will be worth
it all, as you go through. Even if doesn't make sense for
others, but in the end it will make perfect sense.

Change takes action.
Why not start this very moment?
It will be a better tomorrow because of this very moment.
By the actions you take today.
Don't put off until tomorrow what you can do today.
You're one step closer to a brighter tomorrow,
By the choices you make to today.

Chapter 39

The Finish Line

The journey of writing this story took me on an adventure about myself that I didn't know at the time. Some things are best left alone and move on from it. You can't change things that have already happened. It doesn't do any good to dig up the past; it won't last by staying there. It won't change a thing that's already happened.

Let's start again, and let bygones be bygones. Forgiveness takes you to a new place that you've never been before now. The peace you have is the best feeling of all, not carrying around all that excess baggage.

How light and freeing it is to be yourself and not having to pretend that you are happy when you know you are not, by being someone you are not. There is a time in your life when you need to stop running from who you really are and who you would like to be. That is to be free from anger and disappointment. It happens when you take the time and face your inner fears that bring you to tears that you have been running from for way too long. Know the time has come to go for it. Dare to be the real you.

Have the courage to move forward to make a difference in the world around you; it is okay to be you, the person God intended you to be. No need to put yourself through all that nonsense of trying to be perfect in an imperfect world. It is okay; there is no need to be afraid. God is with you, and he will never leave you or forsake you.

Take that leap of faith; God will be there every step you take.
You are special in every way possible.
Believe you are because you are.
Dare to be different, free to be yourself.

You have so much to give, so much to enjoy on your journey ahead of you, it's amazing. We all are part of the big puzzle and part of the game. Play your part of your life; someone has something to learn from it. We need each other to learn and grow. Start today before the day is over and the finish line is getting closer.

Don't waste another moment crying over spilled milk and what others haven't done for you or what they've done to you. Live for the moment you have been given. Have fun with your adventure of a lifetime, your life that you have been given. It's a gift; have fun with your journey you've been living.

Share it with others, the real and wonderful you!
Dare to be different, free to be yourself.
It's only the beginning, not the end.
Till you get to the finish line.

CHAPTER 40

Ending

I have learned a lot about myself as well about others in the process. No one is perfect, and that includes me. Over the years I thought I had to be perfect for everything to be right. In fact, that was all wrong to put myself through all that torture, as well as my family. And for that, I truly am sorry. Hopefully, someday you all will forgive me for the past mistakes. The pressures and all the rushing throughout our lives to be perfect, which wasn't perfect either.

It feels so good to let yourself off the hook from all the screwy little things you put yourself under. I'm letting go of all that nonsense of all that past tense. But time to move onward to brighter and lighter days.

This is me, courageous and bold, and I will not fold. No more being tied up in knots and always throwing fits to always be perfect in an imperfect world, That's in a tailspin, a little out of control. But the truth is, we can operate in self-control. When we hand our lives over to Jesus, he will guide you and me through to be the real you and me.

Don't live in fear. Live out loud.

Life needs to be easygoing. Don't be pressured to be something you're not. We all are on a journey to the same place, to go to heaven. In life right now, you can live in God's presence. Each and every day you can open your heart, and let God in.

Your adventure of a lifetime starts as soon as you invite Jesus into your heart. He starts his transformation of a lifetime. It is amazing what he can do, and what he does for one, he will do for another. You will not be left out unless you chose to be. The party of a lifetime awaits you. Don't be afraid to step out of the boat and get up and get going once again.

When doubt comes into your mind, send it packing without regret. Simply believe and trust you will soon see life is an adventure. Why sit idle as your life passes you by?

Get back in the game, and play all the innings of your game with you in mind, not what others think you need to play when it is your game to play. We all have dreams and positions laid out for us to play. We are all wanted, and we won't let you forget it.

Listen to your heart, even when it gets broken, as it does from time to time. It takes time to heal, and as the scars begin to heal, it's comforting to know it will be okay in time.

When you get down in the dumps and feel stumped, and you don't know what to do, don't give up on your dreams, even when you fall. Get up and go again. That makes us who we are every time we get up and go once again.

The only time you get defeated is when you stay down. That's when your hope is all gone. You've taken your focus off God, and you don't know what to do. The first thing is to put it right back in his direction.

It's the only way for things to get better. When your problems are too big for you to handle, call on God; he is much bigger than your problems will ever be. He always has an answer to each of them and a solution to get you through each of them.

You will be able to come out stronger than you were in them. So when you see someone else struggling the way you've been, send a prayer up for him or her. Help others when you can. If you need help, ask a friend to lend a helping hand. Life is about helping each other when you can. Encourage them when they get discouraged and have lost all hope. Don't give up on others when darkness seem to fade into their eyes. When their hope is all gone, that's when they need you the most. Don't coast through life and just think of yourself. Think of others more than yourself, and your life will have more meaning. Be there more and more, and show them how much you really care. Don't just say that you care, but show them how much.

Others don't care what you are selling or what you are all about until you show them how much you really care.

About caring for others and putting others needs above your own—it shows what's in your heart and how far you will go to help someone. Your motive shows what character is all about. Know what you are all about. You have don't have to act like someone else. God has a place for each one of us. We all have a part to play in his plan. It's a game that we all can win, but first you need to get into game.

We are all unique in every way possible.

Don't try to change the things that make you special in every way. If we need changing, God will do it. Celebrate your uniqueness. We all have a gift that needs to be played in our game of life. We are all on a journey. Face your fears and leave them in the dirt of the rear of the steer. The dust has put up such a fuss that it makes you want to cuss.

The faith that you have will give you the strength to leave it in the dust of the past at last. Won't go there once it's gone, the fear that has held you back long enough. Being afraid is the reason that you haven't stepped forward until now.

Your boat has been docked long enough. It is time to take up the anchor and go forward. With the steps that have been laid out for you, it's time to take that step you have been dreaming of doing. After the long looks of test and trials of time, why are you still in the same spot that you were yesterday?

Yesterday is gone; the future is today, the moment you can take.

Don't wait until the end of your life, wishing you had done what you have always wanted to do. The end is now. Why not start today and get back into the game? Don't be afraid. God is with you every step of the way. Take the moment you have been given, and start living. Go for it. Enjoy your life; try new adventures, things that you have always wanted to do.

The time is now; your life has just begun, the adventure of a lifetime.

Dare to be different, free to be yourself! Don't let anyone tell you any different; listen to your heart. When others object, it's because they are too afraid to go after their own dreams. Being bold takes courage to go after what you truly believe in. We all have dreams and goals in mind. No more living out what others think and say what you should do or not do. It's up to you, not them. Do not listen to the Negative Nellies. Grab hold of the Positive Pollies.

When others talk about you, they are afraid of what you are doing because they cannot do what you are doing. You are living and loving out loud. Being the real you takes courage. You are uniquely and divinely made the way God wanted you to be, so don't be afraid. You have nothing to prove by being you!

Have fun, and enjoy your adventure of a
lifetime. Get back into the game!

Dare to be different, free to be yourself!

This book is about how you can overcome obstacles. The fears throughout the years will take some tears to get past them. It takes courage to live out loud the love we have in our hearts. No one is perfect, and we don't need to act like we are in order to be accepted. Let go of the past, and move onward to the future. Stand strong, even when you go wrong. Soon it will be okay once again. Put your trust and belief in Jesus. He is here to help us and to guide us through life—to dare to be different, free to be yourself. It's okay to be different, to stand out in a crowd. You will be seen by the things you do and say.

Learn to keep moving forward and stay in the game of life. Help others along the way, being led by the heavenly Father, without being afraid of what others might say. Keep doing what is right, even if it feels wrong. But keep doing it; it will pay off down the road.

The light will shine bright in our hearts tonight without fright, only delight in sight. The kite that is in flight is for everyone's delight. On your bike through the streets and as you climb the hills, peddle through the raindrops that fall from the sky. Keep moving forward, and you will see a brighter tomorrow. Our dreams are closer than you think. Go out, and you can get them. Start moving, and your adventure begins. Have fun along the way. Try something new each day!

Put a smile on someone's face as you run your race. Love out loud!

Printed in the United States
By Bookmasters